to my husband,
Ian Montgomery

Joy Hendry, born 1953 Perth, educated Perth Academy and Edinburgh University (MA in Mental Philosophy). First poem pubished in the school magazine, *The Young Barbarian*, in 1967. Cut folk-singing teeth at Perth and Crieff and other surrounding folk clubs. Teacher of English, 1977-84. Editor since 1971 of Scottish literary magazine, *Chapman*, Since 1984, freelance writer: poet, playwright, theatre critic and broadcaster, radio critic of *The Scotsman*. Writer in Residence for Stirling District Council 1991-3. Editor of critical volumes on Norman MacCaig and Sorley MacLean. Literary publisher, including *The Diary of a Dying Man*, Soutar's valedictory diary. Her radio play about William Soutar, *The Wa' at the Warld's End* (a different play from *Gang Doun*, not an adaptation) broadcast on Radio 4 in October 1993, and a distillation for children's radio of Soutar's life broadcast in *The Story and the Song* series for Radio Scotland 1992.

Gang Doun wi a Sang

A play about William Soutar

by

Joy Hendry

diehard
Edinburgh
mxmv

diehard
publishers
3 Spittal Street
Edinburgh
EH3 9DY

ISBN 0 946230 25 0

British Library Cataloguing in Publication Data
  A catalog record for this book is
  available from the British Library

The publisher acknowleges the financial assistance of the Scottish
Arts Council in the publication of this volume.

Other **diehard** drama

Klytemnestra's Bairns, Bill Dunlop
Hare and Burke, Owen Dudley Edwards
Port and Lemon, the mystery behind Sherlock Holmes/*Laird
  of Samoa*, John Cargill Thompson
Cheap and Tearful/Feel Good, John Cargill Thompson
A Matter of Conviction/Parting Shot/When the Rain Stops,
  John Cargill Thompson

currently at the printers

The Lord Chamberlain's Sleepless Nights, a collection of
  plays by John Cargill Thompson
*Hamlet II Prince of Jutland/Macbeth Speaks/An English
  Education*, John Cargill Thompson
Alcestis, by George Buchanan

INTRODUCTION

Gang Doun wi a Sang celebrates the life and work of William Soutar (1898–1943) Perth poet, who has left us such a wonderful body of writing: poetry in Scots and English, including the bairnrhymes, his diaries, journals, letters and other writings. The facts of his life, contracting when still a young man a spondylitic condition, in which the vertebrae of his spine gradually locked in a rigid position, becoming more restricted in movement and finally confined to bed for his last 13 years, tempt one to look at him as a tragic figure. But Soutar coped with illness with great dignity and courage, and without losing his pawky, wry sense of humour.

The play is based on Soutar's own writings, from diaries, letters, journals, dream books, the poems, and on reminiscences from some who knew him, family and friends. Many of the words are Soutar's (or MacDiarmid's) own, although adapted for dramatic purposes. I have tried to give dramatic life to the mind of the poet which was free to roam even though his body was imprisoned by infirmity.

My main means of achieving this is through two actors playing Soutar, although otherwise the part would be so big as to be difficult for any actor to cope with. Briefly, Soutar A in the first act represents the spirit, the essence, the eternal character of Soutar, while Soutar B enacts in more or less naturalistic mode the biographical progession of Soutar's life. In the second act, they are reversed, with Soutar A enacting the life while Soutar B acts as his spirit and commentator. Audiences can read as much as they like into this: certainly there is a sense of the spirit Soutar, whether A or B, acting as Virgil-like guide to the development of the poet. I have also included Soutar's writings, his poems and diary entries, almost as characters and scenes in the drama: they were, after all, the most important events in his life.

Soutar spoke with a Perthshire accent and wrote much poetry in Scots, but most of his prose, which was my main source material, was written in English. Consequently there was a temptation to translate all of it into 'Synthetic Scots' – the literary dialect of Scots used by many modern writers of the language –

and by Soutar himself. I have resisted this temptation, but nevertheless written the bulk of the dialogue in a light, conversational Scots, such as I imagine Soutar used on a daily basis. My setting out of the Scots dialogue is intended to act as a gentle and by no means prescriptive guide to pronunciation. It is important, though, that the play is not rendered in a Glaswegian Scots, but as far as possible in the Perthshire Scots which was Soutar's native tongue.

My main and fervent hope is that this play does justice to a remarkable man whose life, in fact, is such a moving but in some ways very ordinary story, but whose writing deserves not just national, but international recognition.

I would like to acknowledge the invaluable assistance of the following in the writing of this play: Dr Stanley Simpson and the staff of the National Library of Scotland, W. R. Aitken, the late Alexander Scott, Tom Scott, Soutar's family, especially Mollie MacKenzie and Jess MacKenzie, Jim Guthrie and Perth and Kinross District Libraries and Museums for allowing me for the duration of the play to stay in 27 Wilson Street, Perth, 'Soutar Hoose', gifted to the town by John Soutar after his death and now the home of a writer in residence, Peter Cudmore for looking after the *Chapman* office, John and Janet Law for their continuing interest and support, to Joan Knight, many years artistic director of Perth Theatre, for commissioning me to write a play I wanted to write anyway, and for her invaluable advice and help throughout, and all the actors, especially James Telfer and Liam Brennan, for their enthusiasm.

Gang Doun wi a Sang was first performed at the Perth Citizens Theatre, 12 October 1990, with James Telfer as William Soutar A and Liam Brennan as William Soutar B. Martyn James played John Soutar and Ann Scott-Jones, Margaret Soutar. David Low and Bill MacKenzie were played by Paul Stanfield and Jim Finlayson by Kenneth Lindsay. Professor Herbert Grierson and Hugh MacDiarmid were both played by Alec Heggie, Evelyn Soutar by Becky Baxter, and Mollie MacKenzie by Kate McConnachie. The play was directed by Joan Knight with Ken Alexander as assistant director; designer Nigel Hook, lighting Simon Sewell. Musical settings of the poems were composed by John Scrimger and sung by James Nicol.

PROLOGUE

The stage is completely empty behind a gauze, with the bed flown above. The gauze is lit to suggest the garden outside the window. Soutar A is standing in front of the gauze, Soutar B immediately behind and obscured by him.

Soutar A: The end comes for us aa. For me it cam in the wee smaa hoors. I'm no sure o the time. Aboot two o'clock I asked Mums for a gless o water. She wanted tae bide wi me but I sent her back tae bed – it was cauld – and I thocht the end wis near. I wanted tae slip oot unnoticed. But they wad be listenin. They heard me stirrin last nicht. I wunner gin they heard ma graveyard hoast, or ma hand brushin the sheet, or the creak o the windae as I slipped through and oot intae the gairden beyond ... Movement at last ...

The lights go up on the garden outside, but leaving the room in darkness, a predominant impression of green, the luxuriance of nature. Soutar B moves out from behind him. Sound of birdsong.

Soutar B: Out of the darkness of the womb
Into a bed, into a room:
Out of a garden into a town,
And to a country, and up and down
The earth; the touch of women and men
And back into a garden again:
Into a garden; into a room;
Into a bed and into a tomb;
and the darkness of the world's womb.

Exit Soutar B into the garden.

Soutar A: *(addressing the audience)* 'Womb', 'room', 'tomb'– big words – like 'beginning', 'middle', 'end'. A journey frae derkness oot into the nectar o light; ye drink it in; ye're surrounded by it; it shapes aathin – the trees, the birds and animals, earth, water, fire – room eneuch indeed. I wis juist beginnin tae reach oot and touch life, juist beginnin tae loe men – and women, when derkness grupped me and slowly drew me back. The finger o death is on us aa, but for me it wis a leaden haun that clutched me owre soon.

A bed is like a womb, a room is like a bed – it haps you wi its warmth, it keeps the elements oot. But you can leave yer bed and stap intae the room, ye can leave the room and go oot and roam the yirth like a tinker. But when the bed is yer world, the room yer universe, when your body is its own jailor, then all of it: room, bed, body, become a living tomb. Thirteen years I lay in a bed, the best years o my life – my prime – when I should hae been courtin a wife, beddin her, faitherin bairns, gettin and spendin money, thirteen years ...

Act 1 Scene 1

Bring on simple furniture – a bench and a lectern.

Soutar A: But I wisna born paralysed! Frae the stert I wis a richt wee bugger! I wis as swack a bairn as ye could imagine – a genuine twelve and a half punner – I thudded into the world and no mistake. The doctor said to Mums: "Fetch me a pinafore and we'll pack him off to skule."

Soutar B: Whan Alistair McAlister
Was born at Corsie Hill
The doctor said: "Pit on his breeks
And pack him off to skūle."

Soutar A: But the skule wis nae joke for me. I hatit bein strapped in, tellt whit tae dae, so I rebelled.

Switch to a classroom scene. A teacher is droning on. Soutar B comes up to her.

Soutar B: Miss Morrison, remember me?

Miss Morrison: Wullie Soutar! Could I ever forget you! You were a terrible nuisance. You would not do as you were told. Every time I looked at you your mind was away – aye thinking up mischief, pinging inkblots at the girls, hiding other pupils' jotters.

Soutar B: Sorry about that. I just didnae like bein 'keepit in'. I actually liked you, although I ken you didnae think that.

Miss Morrison: Well, you could've fooled me, right enough. The last straw for me was the time when the class were going through the times tables – each pupil in turn shouting out the answer. When it came your turn, *(she mimics herself):* 'Willie Soutar! What are two threes?'

Soutar B: *(initially making the sound)* Puddocks –

Miss Morrison: Four sixes?

Soutar B: Puddocks –

Miss Morrison: Seven nines?

Soutar B: Puddocks!

Miss Morrison: Do you remember what I did to you for that?

Soutar B: You put me in a desk richt oot at the front, where everythin I did could be seen.

Miss Morrison: Yes – and I belted you. Six of the best.

Soutar B: But you belted me every day.

Miss Morrison: Did I? – oh dear...

The scene fades as Soutar moves away, exit teacher.

Soutar A: The climax o my primary skule career at the Southern District School wis the strike I organised in 1911. Industrial unrest wis rife, miners, dockers, workers aa ower Scotland, downin tools and walkin oot. It wisnae sae muckle us sympathisin wi the strikers but mair o a copy-cat action – strikin sounded like fun. The men struck agin their capitalist overlords, we agin the oppression of the Southern District School!

Enter two 'boys'. They and Soutar B cavort about the stage, playtime fashion.

Soutar B: Hey, lads. I've a great idea! Ken the workers are on strike! They're refusin tae dae whit the gaffers tell them. The miners in Motherwell and Fife, and the Dundee spinners an weavers, they laid doon tools yesterday and merched oot o the pit.

Boy One: Whit fur are they on strike?

Soutar B: They're wantin mair pey and a shorter workin week.

Boy Two: We could dae wi a shorter workin week an' aa.

Soutar B: Like only comin tae skule on Mondays.

Boy Two: Or never comin tae skule at aa!

Soutar B: I get fair seek o jumpin when they bells ring. When yin bell rings ye rin in tae yer cless, an ye're thumped if ye're late. Whan anither bell rings ye git loused for a few magic minutes and then anither bell rings an ye rin back in again. It's pure hell!

Boy One: Ah ken. Ye'd think we wis puppets on a string!

Soutar B: Ay, but if the miners can go on strike, so can we. When the interval bell rings, we'll merch oot o the gates and richt across the South Inch – and no come back when the bell goes – juist stravaig aboot the Inch fur the rest o the day.

They stand up and arrange themselves in order, and set off, singing 'Fall in and follow me, have a banana'.

Soutar A: *(addresses the audience)* So that's whit we did. Whan the bell rang, we marched oot in guid order, singin. But hauf ma army took cauld feet whan they heard the bell ring at the end o interval an ran back into the school.

Boy Two: Hey, Wullie, look! Aa they yellow-belly scardeygoats are turnin tail and rinnin.

Boy One: So they are. Wullie, dae ye no think we should go back too!

Soutar B: Whit a pair o scabs you are. Keep merchin!

Boy Two: Listen, Wullie. I got hell fae my mither yesterday fur gettin intae trouble at skule. The teacher sent me hame wi a note tellin her aboot whit I'd been daein, an I goat thrashed again!

Soutar B: Whaur's yer guts – yer spunk! Well, I suppose mebbe we better gae back in. But nae rinnin back. We'll merch proodly back like sodgers.

All: *(singing)* Fall in and follow me... have a banana!...

The singing fades as there is a clanging of gates as the school gates shut. A stern looking male teacher appears, wielding a tawse with sadistic pleasure.

Boy Two: Jings! It's Charlie Robertson!

Soutar B: And would ye look at yon strap! It's aboot three inches thick!

Boy One: I dinna like the wey he's wavin that in the air!

Robertson: I'm glad to see you boys have some idea of military discipline. It's just a pity you didn't choose a more suitable musical accompaniment. Just what do you think you were trying to do?

Soutar B: *(boldly)* We were going on strike, Sir.

Robertson: On strike, Soutar? Armstrong, you too?

Boy One: *(not quite so boldly)* Well, yes Sir.

Robertson: And what gave you that brilliant idea? Soutar – I suppose you were the 'organiser'.

Soutar B: Yes Sir – the Motherwell miners are on strike, Sir. We thought we'd show some solidarity.

Robertson: Solidarity ... h-hm. Well, now you've crossed your own picket line, I trust you'll be upping tools as well. I hope you're repentant...

Soutar B: No! Sir!

Robertson: Well, Soutar, you're about to feel the solidarity of my belt. The strikers are going to be struck. Good and proper!

Soutar A: And we were, good and proper. *(he blows on his hands and winces at the memory of the pain)*

Soutar A: I uised tae watch the warld go by frae my Grannie's windae, one floor up in the Auld High Street. Here I played ma first trick – an a great ploy it wis too. Ma Grannie had a flooer box on the windae sill and I gaithered hard pieces o earth oot o this, rolled them up intae a wee baa and drapped them doon on unsuspectin passers by. When I scored a hit, I pu'd my heid back in again, an they wad look up wi puzzled stares, rubbin the bit that wis sair! But naethin tae be seen.

Soutar B: No even ootsize seagulls!

Soutar A: But whaur did ma poetry come frae? Somewhaur in the thick o youth, oot o ploys like the school strike. Oot o a delicious feelin o aliveness, as if the very blood would burst my veins. I remember whan I was aboot seiven or eight, leapin alang the Shore Road near the old saw-mill, wi the dust inches deep under my bare feet. Every noo and then I louped up intae the air and brung my feet thegither doon-pointed like a ballet dancer. For yin ecstatic second I was shair – I kent I hovered, still i the air like a hawk, sightin its prey. The moment itsel seemed tae hover, caught in a glisk o eternity. I felt that near unbearable *joi de vivre:* when rinnin on roofs, leapin frae a height and somersaultin in mid-air, or flyin alang a touch-line tae meet an centre a perfectly turned pass. – *(he leaps in the air)* – Ya beauty! But at the hert o ma poetry is the auld burgh of Perth, St Johnstoun. Ken, there isnae a place in Perth whaur ye cannae see a hill: Kinnoull wi its green cleuch, Craigie Knowes wi its whin busses, Buckie Braes whaur monys the lad an lass has dune their coortin. Frae the hill they caa the Burghmuir ye can see the far-aff Grampians, purpie wi heather, or aiblins white wi snaa. It gies ye a feel o the warld's room streitchin oot in front o ye.

Soutar B: Hae ye come in be yon toun
Ablow the craigie knowes?
Hae ye come in be yon toun
Whaur the clear water rows?

Birk and rodden on the brae,
Hawthorn in the hauch;
And clear water churlin by
The elder and the sauch.   *(Exit)*.

Soutar A: At day-daw and at grey-fa'
The merry bells ding doun:

>At day-daw and grey-fa'
>There's music in yon toun.
>
>Merle and mavie whistle clear;
>And whan the hour is still
>Haikers owre the auld brig hear
>The gowk upon the hill.
>
>Wha wudna bide in yon toun
>Ablow the craigie knowes?
>Wha wudna bide in yon toun
>Whaur the clear water rows?

Enter Soutar's mother, young, bustling. Soutar B drops into youthful mode. 'Congregation' on stage.

Margaret Soutar: *(calling out)* – Wullie – are ye no ready yet?

Soutar B: *(reluctantly)* Ay, I'm comin.

Margaret S: We'll be late fur the kirk gin ye dinnae get a muve on.

John Soutar: Ay Willie, we haena missed a Sunday since we were merriet – an we're no startin noo owre you.

Soutar B: I'm no complainin – dinna nag me.

They move into an area of the stage with a pew. The impression should be of a stern Calvanist kirk, bare, no ornament except a simple cross set on a table and a lectern.

Minister: From the day of our creation, sin has eaten into our flesh and bone. Eve was tempted by the serpent to eat of the fruit of the tree of knowledge, God banished Adam and Eve from the Garden of Eden, to tread the dusty, thorny paths of this world. And since then no man has been without sin, and we are all doomed to an eternity of hell-fire and damnation.

Soutar B: *(fidgeting moodily in his seat – aside)* He makes God sound gey nasty, if ye ask me.

Margaret S: *(shaking him)* Willie – stop fidgeting.

Soutar B: Sorry, mither.

Minister: We must all strive after the godly life, to walk in the paths of righteousness. Consider the lilies of the fields: they toil not, neither do they spin. Take no thought for the morrow for our destiny lies in the Lord's hands. God is like a stern father. He sees our sinfulness, knows our innermost thoughts. And we will have to account for our smallest transgressions before the Lord on

Judgement Day. There will be no escape.

Soutar has fallen asleep. His mother nudges him again. Thinking he is on the football field instead of in the kirk, he begins to kick out at the pew in front, first with one foot, then with the other. He shouts out "Goal!"

Margaret S: *(angry)* Willie – stop that! Where do you think you are?

John Soutar: Willie – I will speak to you later.

Soutar B: *(muttering recalcitrantly)* Yon meenister's like a bad tempered bull. *(he sits moodily and restlessly in the pew, taking care not to fall asleep again).*

Minister: There is but one hope, that by the grace of God ye may be admitted into the company of the Elect – the chosen few of God, ordained to remain with him in paradise. Be ye therefore humble before him, remembering ye are dust, defiled with sin ... *(Soutar B is still muttering restlessly)* ...The blessing of God Almighty, the power of the holy spirit, be with you always, now and forever, Amen.

Soutar B: Thank God for that!

John Soutar: Right, my lad – you're for it.

Margaret and John Soutar hustle Willie out of the church. They move to another part of the stage – representing home.

John Soutar: Willie, ye've tae learn tae respect the word of the Lord. There's naethin mair important in life. He is the way, the truth an the life.

Margaret S: That's right. The Lord is your Shepherd.

Soutar B: Ay, but he's no ma jailor!

John Soutar: *(sternly, asserting his authority)* Say nae mair! Here, tak yer punishment. Be gratefu that it isnae waur nor this. *(he takes a bottle of castor oil, uncorks it)* Mums – get me a spuin, please.

Margaret S: Here ye are. *(hands him a horn spoon)*

John Soutar: Ye're lucky I dinna believe in thrashin bairns, but I'll gie ye a bittie discomfort to learn ye proper behaviour. Here – tak three moothfu's o this.

Soutar B: Ugh – oh well, I suppose there's naethin for it. *(he complies).*

John Soutar: Right – go to your bed.

Soutar exits, moodily and not at all contrite.

Margaret S: I doot oor son's no mindfu o the fear o the Lord. We'll hae tae be mair strict wi him.

John Soutar: Ay, but it's difficult. He's got that muckle independent spirit.

Margaret S: I ken – John. I mind yin day whan he wis aboot three or fower – Willie an me wis walkin doon alang Tay Street, an I had a hud o his haund. I noticed that Wullie had a richt black glower on his face. When he saw me luikin doon at him, he wrenched his haund awa and teetered on ahead on his wee legs. Whan I tried tae rin an catch him, he shouted at me like a stern school dominie: "Get back, get back. I do not require a mother!"

John Soutar: Ay, I mind ye tellin me o that.

Margaret S: Weel, I wis taken aback bi his adult words and tone of voice, no tae say a bittie hurt, him sayin he didna need me an aa, but I kent it wis his prood nature, and that ma son wis nae ordinary laddie.

John Soutar: Mebbe so, but I wish he'd behave himsel – in the kirk at least!

Soutar A: Despite my moody Sabbath rebelliousness, and the minister impressing fear intae aa these souls, the sheer drama o't inspired me. Yin day when I was aboot three year auld – we were veesitin ma Grannie efter Sunday mornin service. I louped up ontae a stool ahint the kitchen door and gied them aa a sermon, standin there, waggin ma young heid in the pu'pit. But whan I wis in full evangelical flight, the Lord got his ain back: the door ahint me opened and Grannie cam in and knocked me fleein!

But the ministry wisnae fur me. Aa that darkness and damnation. The love o the flesh burned bricht in me and nae amount o hellfire could pit it oot. But there was a guid side tae it: the hoors listenin tae sermons gied me an ear for rhetoric and argument, and the cadences of the psalms gied me the rhythms for my verse...

Company sing as a congregation the following to the tune of 'The Old Hundred' – all people that on earth –

> Lift up your e'en and greet nae mair,
> The black trees on the brae are still;
> And lichtsome, in the mirkl'd air
> A star gangs glaidly owre the hill.

> Sae far awa fae worldly soun'
> In laneliness it glimmers by;
> And the cauld licht comes kindly doun
> On earth and a' her misery.   *(Exit)*.

Soutar A: In those pews – "at the breist o the laft' – I composed ma first poem. I thocht it impressive and 'elevating'. Yin line was very like Tennyson –

Soutar B: "stepping stones of our dead lives to higher things"

Soutar A: *(apologetically)* I wis about 15 or 16 at the time and felt shair I'd improved on the auld master. I mind playin fitbaa in the shadda o St. Leonards in the Fields. I got sae cerriet away wi the exertion o the game that I cried oot:

Soutar B: "O Christ!"

Soutar A: That stopped me in ma tracks – I'd committed the unforgivable sin o blasphemy. The dark haund o the kirk is hard tae shak aff. But I played wi sic virr that yin day the dominie said tae me, "Man, Soutar, you leap about like the very devil".

Soutar B: So the energy o the deil won the day.

Soutar A: Yince at Perth Academy, I began tae enjoy school. Some teachers were a real inspiration, like George MacKinlay, a poet with sic love of words that I became quite infected by it.

Soutar B settles himself into a school desk. MacKinlay enters and begins to teach with obvious enthusiasm.

MacKinlay: Never underestimate the power of words. It is fine to be strong and fit, to run, to leap, to use tools, make things, but you can go places with words that you can never go in real life. Words and imagination can take you from the humblest cottage to the grandest palace in the twinkling of a thought. And poetry – poetry is the distilled essence of words, synthesising meaning and idea, intellect and feeling, image and sound... *(Soutar B is absorbed in this, visibly excited. He puts up his hand)* Yes, Soutar?

Soutar B: Have you read my poem in the school magazine, Sir.

MacKinlay: Er, yes – a bit facetious, I thought 'The Academy Boy' – not much romantic inspiration there.

Soutar B: Well, OK sir, but I've written anither yin ye micht like a bit better.

MacKinlay: Would you like to read it out to us?

Soutar B: *(recites poem)*

> Give me a fire and four grey walls,
> A fire and an old time chest,
> The hour when the shrieking owl calls,
> And the crow has gone to rest.
>
> Then can I conjure up strange scenes,
> Brave legends of long ago,
> And see the crude and dancing fiends
> As they flitter to and fro.
>
> Some seem so real, some seem so gay
> That I've hopes that they are there,
> When dreamily they fade away,
> Into realms beyond the air.

MacKinlay: Good, Soutar. Better than the other effort. You handle the stanza form and the rhyme quite confidently. But do you imagine these 'strange scenes'? Are they real to you?

Soutar B: Oh yes, Sir. When I'm reading Greek mythology, I feel it's for real – happening in front of my eyes. I see Venus rising from the faem like a fisherman pu'in a salmon oot o the Tay. When you mention 'John Knox' to me, I see a large and grim pulpit rising above me, and the man himsel, stern and awfae, wi his great grey beard, thumpin awa in the pulpit.

MacKinlay: That's interesting. Well, keep at it. We might make a poet oot o ye yet. *(a bell rings)* That's all for now. Class dismissed. *(the class rise. Soutar B goes out with Mackinlay, still talking about poetry).* I'll show you my poems one day, if you like.

Soutar A: At last my energies fand an outlet in school activities insteid o causin trouble. I jined the Boy Scouts. Whan war broke out in 1914, I jined the School Cadet corps and reached the rank of Sergeant, no less! And I loved sports – I was guid at the high jump – won it at the school sports in 1916 – and a fair hand at the lang leap and putting the stone. I got sae strang I liftit Auntie Bessie frae Orkney aff the grund wi my teeth! She was a wee bit startled.

It's strange how poetry and girls hit you at the same time – about then I began to be overwhelmingly thrilled by the sicht o a shapely ankle. A beautiful leg quite turned my heid.

Enter Girl, this time wearing black silk stockings – she is in mourning. Willie stares admiringly at her legs, then realising what the black means, adjusts his expression.

Soutar B: *(trying not to show he's smitten by her, trying to be sympathetic and respectful)* Daisy, how are you all getting on? How's your mum?

Daisy: She's bearing up not too badly. Since Dad was killed on the Western Front there's been so much for her to do, keeping the house going, she hasn't much time to fret. We all miss him so much, though. *(she stifles a sob).*

Soutar B: I'm sorry. There's not much you can say that's a comfort.

Daisy: I know. Don't worry about it.

Soutar B: *(brightening up)* Daisy – I was going to take a stroll tonight – up to Cherrybank, maybe up Buckie Braes and Callerfountain. Would you like to come with me?

Daisy: *(doubtful at first, but looking at Soutar and beginning to show interest)* Well, I don't think my mother would really mind. You can't stay sad forever.

Soutar B: Meet you at the South Street Port at seven o'clock.

Daisy: OK. *(Daisy goes out)*

Soutar A: She was a bit late. I thought she had changed her mind, but, after about ten minutes, she came running up, breathless. Before long we were walking up into the little rocky gully of Buckie Braes.

Soutar B: *(to Daisy as they stroll along together)* I love this place – the trees, beech, rowan, ash, cliffs to climb, if you've a mind, or you can cook sausages on a fire in the crannies in the rock.

Daisy: Ay, and there's always the sky above – and the stars. It all seems so huge and silent.

Soutar B: And us so tiny down below. Watch noo, here's the burn. Gie me your haund and I'll help ye across.

He does so. There is silence as he holds on to her hand. She wonders whether to withdraw it, decides not to. Soutar kisses her, gently, shyly. They embrace. After a bit they walk on.

Daisy: Do you write a lot of poetry?

Soutar B: I'm trying tae. I dinna ken if it's up tae onythin', but I've a feeling I'll write something really guid one day. Maybe I'll write a poem for you...

They stand, facing each other, holding both hands. Enter a reader.

Reader: I have known women fonder far
Than you; more fair, more kind;
Women whose passionate faces are
Flowers in the mind:
But as a tall tree, stem on stem,
Your presence overshadows them.

They can but copy all I found
When you alone grew in this ground.

They release hands. Daisy turns and goes off. Soutar watches her as she goes.

Soutar B: *(addressing Daisy, though she's no longer there)*
...And my sleep shall be sweet with the thought
That thy love is to me as a star,
With flower-scent and moonlight fraught,
And the laughter of children afar:
When thy name wings to me subtle gleams
Of still waters where calm shadows are –
Only in dreams... *(exit Soutar B)*

Soutar A: Ay, those black silk stockings haunted ma dreams until ma dying day...

1916 is my halcyon year – I wis 18 year auld – my last year at Perth Academy. Then I kent fully whit it wis tae be young and alive. I wis yin o the fleetest and strongest at the Academy: first in ma year at maist things: I was writing poetry: I was in love, popular in the classroom and on the playing-field: I never reached that peak of living fullness again.

But the shadow o the war wis there, and it showed in unexpected weys. The afternuin Kitchener's death was made public, I was crossin the North Inch where some senior boys were practisin putting the weight for the sports. Somebody tellt me Kitchener had been drowned, which galvanised me into mindless exuberance, and I set aff towards the athletes, leapin and runnin and shoutin, "Hurrah! Kitchener's dead!" Then, wi aa o them starin at me, I picked up the weight and gied it a michty heave, outdistancing aa the previous throws. Whit I wis really saying

was: "Look! Death, look! Here is somebody alive and very much
alive".

Soutar A goes out. Spotlight on the bed.

Act 1 Scene 2

Reader: Ho! I joined the Royal Navy
When I had little sense;
But I came home with rheumatics
And a lot of experience.

He looks at the bed.

'Ballad of a Not So Able-Bodied Seaman' *(Exit).*

Enter Soutar A.

Soutar A: I left school in December, 1916 – my last contribution
was to the school magazine – a poem – 'War'

Soutar B: *(begins to declaim the poem in a melodramatic style)*
But a mighty god roamed o'er that strand,
With Titan strides he stalked the plain
And shook aloft, with might and main,
A glittering shield in his brawny hand...
And softly on the breeze were borne
The fading thrummerings of war.

He finishes the poem with a grand gesture.

Soutar A: *(who has been watching with amusement)* Of course, it
was just like that...

*A nautical scene. Bare room with table. Soutar is marched on by a
petty officer.*

Officer: OK, Ordinary Seaman Soutar. I've shown you round the
H.M.S. Eclipse, so now you'll be an expert, eh?

Soutar B: *(hesitantly)* Yes Sir. I've just one question. Where do I
sleep?

Officer: Use your imagination, Soutar. Your initiative.

Soutar B: *(looks around in disbelief)* But where do the rest of the
men sleep?

Officer: Dunno. Hanging from the mast, I expect.

Soutar B: But I haven't seen anything that looks like a dormitory, or bunks.

Officer: Crikey, what do you want: a lacy boudoir... ? Tell ya what, ye can doss in here.

Soutar B: In here? But on what?

Officer: You recruits is all the same. Is it a bloody feather mattress you're after? Now look at this 'ere table: what's wrong wif that? And yer behind'll make as good a mattress as any, to judge by the look o ye.

Soutar B: *(ignoring the insult)* It seems a bit primitive to me.

Officer: Primitive, eh? Trouble with education − makes ya soft. I'll tell ya, sleepin in 'ere is magic compared to the gun room. 'The Trenches', the men all call it. And do ya know why?

Soutar B: No.

Officer: Because the trenches in a blizzard couldn't be colder. Ya sleep on the stone cold floor covered with a blanket − if ye're lucky.

Soutar B: No wonder the whole ship's splutterin wi the cauld.

Officer: That's nothin! Chaps've been found dead in there. But don't you worry. It's January now − soon be spring time! *(he gives Soutar a paternal pat on the shoulder)*.

Soutar B: *(looks round, shivering)* So it's the table then?

Officer: *(nods complacently)* Ye'll get a blanket from the store.

Soutar B: What about a pillow?

Officer: *(points at Soutar's boots)* These'll do. Nice 'n soft − even give ya a hole ta put your ear in, eh? *(He exits)*.

Soutar A: The navy made me work hard: swabbin the decks, paintin the timbers, shiftin shells, supplies, coals. Some days I lost a full pint of sweat. At last, after months, I wis drafted and, thrilled to my blood, set sail for Nova Scotia tae join H.M.S. Carnarvon at sea. On that day, June 8th, 1917, I felt I'd become a man, and, tae mark the occasion, I began a diary. *(He holds a tiny pocket diary)* What is life if it cannot be remembered.

Soutar B: *(writing letters)* ...The mental stagnation here is simply heartbreaking. All this week I've done nothin but wash down paint work or sand and scrub decks. For maist o these chaps, the want of 'head' work winna bother them, but to chaps like masell it is anither form o starvation..

Soutar A: *(sarondically aside)* What it is to be a genius!

Enter another two sailors.

First Sailor: My back is aching with shifting these sodding shells. Been at it all fuckin afternoon.

Second Sailor: Ay, and tomorrow it's the coal ship – howking all that filthy stuff into the hold, the stour getting in yer lungs. Sooner this war is over, the better I'll be pleased!

Soutar B: *(looking up from his writing)* Well, it's been four years now – and there's no sign of an end to it.

First S: Every time we go back home I notice a difference somewhere. Last time it was my favourite woods where I used ta play as a nipper – all gone ta buggery.

Soutar B: I've just been writing home about that –

Second S: No good at writing letters meself. Can't think of anything to say.

First S: Letters from home aren't always full of comfort and joy – mine read more like a casualty list.

Soutar B: I ken, too many lads I know – from school – or people who worked wi my faither – 'Gone West' shot tae hell in the trenches – and the high heidyins couldnae gie a monkeys.

First S: Ay, how many of them have been near a trench?

Second S: Or stepped on board anything bigger than a rowing boat?

First S: Never mind lads. Remember the old slogan: Are We Downhearted?

All: *(grimly)* No, bloody no.

Soutar B: *(To lift the despondency)* Here, I came across this the other day. *(Digs in pocket for a scrap of paper)* It's the Latest War News. *(The other two groan)* Listen... *(he announces portentously)* It is reported that the enemy have taken Cascara Sagrada.

First S: Ye what?

Soutar B: *(with deliberate pretension and accompanying rude gestures where appropriate)* The enemy have taken CASCARA SAGRADA *(mimes a wee fandango)* – and are making for the DYKES. The British War Office whilst admitting the taking of CASCARA doubt the ability of the enemy to HOLD IT. They are reported to be EVACUATING all along the line and the STRAIN on the REAR is tremendous. The enemy have tried to SUPPRESS this but it has LEAKED OUT *(the others grimace)* at several places and they now know the value of – A SCRAP OF PAPER.

The others roar with laughter

Soutar B: *(finishing)* PRESS BUREAU – PASSED BY THE CENSOR.

First Sailor: I wouldn't mind passing the censor through my arse for what he did to my last letter home.

Soutar B exits and gets into wheelchair. Switch to scene with Soutar writing home: it is now the end of the war.

Soutar A: *(reading from diary)* 11 November 1918 *(pause)* – a day to remember – Peace at last. I went ashore and quite enjoyed myself, flags flying everywhere and people happy and contented. We held a concert aboard at night and every ship celebrated. Bells were ringing, sirens hooting and a fearful row from all over...

Soutar B: But the most important event for me (selfishly, perhaps) is the resuming of my studies...

Soutar A: *(aside)* Self-important ass!...

Soutar B in chair with a cage arrangement over his legs and lamps around it. Enter Sailors One and Two.

First S: Hey, Soutar, what are you doing in that? Fine thing to wait till the war's over and then go sick. I always knew ye couldna stand the bleedin strain!

Second S: I've brought down these letters. I think they're from your folks.

Soutar B: Thanks a lot, chaps.

First S: So what's wrong with you, ye lanky malingerer?

Soutar B: Search me. My feet are throbbing – the Doc's a cretinous old fogey who pokes my feet and goes away muttering. He hasn't a bloody clue. He tells me the treatment is to be hot air baths.

First S: Turkish baths for the sick! Trust you to land in bloody clover! What's it they call it in Sweden, saunas or something!

Second S: And what on earth is this cage arrangement with these funny lamps – man, you look like a building site – or a road works.

Soutar B: Your guess is as good as mine. But I'm shair they'll set fire to the bed – or burn my toes off – some trivial thing like that.

First S: With that great cage affair over yer legs ye look like a baby in a pram...

Soutar B: It's worse that that! They tell me I've not to move a finger's length without a crutch.

Second S: And are you doing as you're told?

Soutar B: Not bloody likely. I don't want to be mistaken for a Mons hero or a Q-boat survivor! All I want to do is to get out of this Navy and into University!

Second S: There goes the professor again. Hey, Bert was tellin me you had a poem published in that magazine ye've always got yer nose into. What's it called?

First S: *(ironically)* 'Great Thoughts'

Soutar B: With friends like you two...

> For the sower must reap of the good seed sown
> And reap of the bad seed too:
> And oh! for the brave intentions flown
> When the breeze of the world blew:

Second S: Willie, ye've sure got a way with words.

First S: Ye're away with words, if ye ask me!

Soutar B: It's my poetic soul!

The First Sailor blows a loud raspberry and hits Soutar a friendly dunt on the shoulder. A nurse wheels him off.

Reader: Yes! I joined the Royal Navy
> When the brass-necked bugles blew;
> And before I came back to my own countrie
> I had learned a thing or two.

> I didn't mind the wind and the rain
> And the hauling on the rope:
> I didn't mind the salty splurge
> And the caustic in the soap

> But who would have thought that an honest man
> Ere he went to fight for the king
> Would stand like a kid with his trousers down
> And salute with his thingummy thing
> Ho Yes! They make your little John Tom
> Take his bonnet off to the King.

Lights dim. Soutar A comes down to address the audience.

Soutar A: I felt stultified in the navy, but it wis ma first – an last – trip intae the world at large. I wis 20 year auld. If I'd never been in the navy, I'd hae missed that vital contact wi ordinary folk and common conditions – minglin in the real community – that was a legacy giftit tae me only once...

Act 1 Scene 3

The backdrop of an Edinburgh skyline

Soutar A: It wis wonderful to enter the halls of Academe, my alma mater, the venerable University of Edinburgh, with its Golden Boy atop the Old College dome. I wrote this in my diary on the first day, 19th April, 1919:

Soutar B: "Remember to seize every opportunity".
"Reverence Truth, Chastity and Love".

Soutar A: Well, a wee bit pompous, perhaps. I studied medicine at first.

Cut to an anatomy class: Soutar B and Soutar's friend, David Low, proudly waving an arm

David: Here's the arm – I managed to 'amputate' it after a bit of a struggle. You've got to get your knife right into the joint and give it a bit of a twist: *(he demonstrates)*

Soutar B: *(grueing)* You get a medal for doing it, but I'll hit you if you don't stop talking about it...

David: If we just lay it on this table, we can inspect it thoroughly.

Soutar B: Did you know that the word 'muscle' is derived from the Latin, meaning 'a little mouse'. You can see why – the muscles look a bit like little rodents.

David: Well, I'm not so hot on the words as you are, but I've got a better grasp of how all the parts of anatomy actually work than you'll ever have, old fruit. Now, here is the elbow joint – the articulation between the humerus, radius and ulna: the great sigmoid cavity of the ulna is adapted...

Soutar B: Enough – don't deafen me with science. *(loosening his tie)* – God! I wish it wasn't so hot! *(sniffing)* Our arm is beginning to 'hum' a bit.

David: Yes, there's a strong resemblance between this anatomy room and a Western Front battlefield.

Soutar B: Jimmy was saying to me that his 'part' was so ripe i t looked as if it could burst into song, or run away.

David: Who's being gruesome now?

Soutar B: I don't think medicine's for me, somehow. There's too much sheer memorising of facts, thousands of them. My brain hurts with it all.

David: It's certainly what I want to do. These stiffs don't bother me. I just think about what I can do for humanity at the end of it.

Soutar B: *(mocking)* Mo-dest-ee!! I think literature is more my thing. I'm signing on for English next term.

David: That'll be better for your poetry, won't it.

Soutar B: *(doubtfully)* I hope so – so long as the course isnae too dry.

David: Do I see you limping a bit. I thought you'd got over that illness of yours?

Soutar B: Well, to tell you the truth, I feel I should be dissected and supplied wi new parts myself. The pains in my hip joint and down the side of my leg are somethin awful. I think it's neuritis. I'm getting massage for it. Otherwise I'm fine, old chap, still hale enough tae gie you a hard time.

David: *(doubtful)* You keep an eye on that. I don't like the sound of it.

Soutar B: Dinna you worry – I've owre mony ambitions tae neglect ma health – anyway – back to this bit of meat. *(Exits with the arm).*

David: *(addressing the audience, with Soutar A listening intently).* Ay, Willie, I was worried about you. Sometimes, even then, I could see the pain in your eyes, catch you limping, favouring your right leg, – when you thought I wasn't looking. I thought then it was more than you and the quacks knew. I've maybe not been much better, but I hope I've made you a bit more comfortable, at least. And all that time, Willie, I never once heard you complain, never once saw you in a temper..

Exit David.

Soutar A: That illness never left me. Then I thocht it wis neuritis – a scurvy varlet – I felt him in ma bones in the mornin – but by night-time he wis gone – until the next morning. And on the rainy days *(shivers)* – he wis in his element.

Now I switched tae English. It wis bliss tae be lat loose amang the best English poets – Keats, Shelley and the rest. Prof. Grierson was an expert on John Donne – that wis a revelation tae me. I was brocht at least three times tae the Delectable Mountains: when I heard the lyrics o Donne: the odes o Wordsworth an Chaucer's 'Pardoner's Tale'.

Enter Soutar B, notebook in hand.

Soutar B: If anything demands from man the best of his speech, of his brain and soul, it is Poetry. She is desired above aa women, a mistress commanding all her lover's heart, a goddess, image and being o the maist beautiful, searching and divine. The refinings of heart and spirit must be dedicated upon her altar.

Soutar A: *(wincing)* The hot air of youth! Like many young romantics, I was haunted by visions of beauty of the "throbbing threnody" of nature, and prompted by ideals of Love and Truth. And I had poems published in the Varsity magazine – *The Student.*

Enter Mother and Father

Mother & Father:

> Leaves, leaves, in moonlit hollows hiding:
> Leaves, leaves, remember ye the Spring?
> Leaves, leaves, on troubled waters riding,
> Tell me your last, lone harbouring.

> Leaves, leaves, in wondrous circles weaving;
> Dance ye for Death, or for the Spring?
> Leaves, leaves, the windswept forests leaving,
> Tell me your last, low whispering.

> Leaves, leaves, in dew-wet rain lying:
> Leaves, leaves, new leaves upon the tree.
> Life, Death, the living and the dying,
> Pledges of Immortality.

Exit Father. Mother in spotlight.

Soutar A: Poor Mums. She wis no mean scribbler herself – it wis frae her that I inherited my gift for words and poetry – and, flushed wi ma intellectual elevation, I uised tae gie her the benefit o my educated opinion on her ain poems.

Soutar B: "You have strained your Pegasus too far and one can hear him shuffling along... Writing poetry, though a serious occupation for some, need not be so for those who write merely for their own little circle and their own pleasure. Most of us like to scribble away, but he who aims at a place among the immortals must build the foundations of his 'Temple of Art' with the utmost care, before he can erect a superstructure to rise above time and space".

Soutar A: *(with a shrug)* Whit can I say? *(changing the subject)* Studying English poetry made me self conscious aboot the poetry I wrote at school and in the Navy. One day, I threw maist o it in the fire – a curious feeling, watchin the pages burn, the words disappearin forever...

Enter Soutar B, dressed in a lavender flowery waistcoat and a noticeably conspicuous tie. With him is another university friend, James Finlayson.

Finlayson: My oath, Bill, but you do look a poet the day!

Soutar B: But Finnel, I'm a poet every day. *(he pulls a paper from his pocket)* Here's my latest effort. Do you remember in the *Scotsman* last week there wis a strange case reported aboot a chap – a young man – dressed tae the nines in his best suit – found dead in the woods out at Flotterston. That picture's been haunting me ever since.

Company:

> We found him dead in the moonlit wood,
> With a lady's scarf across his face;
> And Devereaux spoke of the solitude
> And the weirdness of the place
> And Devereaux understood.
>
> I left the wood and I left the dead -
> A lovers' quarrel, the world would say -
> A tatter'd scarf well smeared with red
> Where the body of Devereaux lay
> With scornful words in his head.
>
> But ofttimes, when sadden'd and all alone
> I finger some shreds of filmy lace,
> And dream of the bodies overgrown,
> And the hatred in *one* dead face.
> Would t'God! he had never known!

Finlayson: Hmmm. I think I'd like tae paint that, somehow.

Soutar B: What excited me was the look on his face. I wish he could have died without knowing he'd been betrayed. Just think –

to go into eternity with that creeping loathing in your soul.

Finlayson exits, leaving Soutar B sitting at his desk, writing.

Soutar B: Today has been a noble day. Finnel and I went for a long walk. The 'toon' looked splendid and the castle hung above the haze like a vision of long ago – Jim waxed eloquent over it and wandered awa intae fantastic realms of thought and imagination. We would paint and sing of the gods of the rivers and mountains and seas... *(he exits)*

During this speech, enter two typical students, naïve but obviously well off. A Jean-Brodie Morningside accent would be appropriate here. They watch him go.

Student 1: Fancies himself, doesn't he? Just look at that ridiculous waistcoat.

Student 2: He's the one that's writes these bombastic and incomprehensible poems in *The Student*. He's always on about his time in the Navy.

Student 1: I just wish these ex-forces students would forget it. I just want to have fun. That's the only thing I'm concerned with. That and doing just enough work to stop Daddy cutting my allowance.

Student 2: My father's promised me a car if I get through my exams in June.

Student 1: You'd better do some work then!

Student 2: Not likely – he'll give it to me anyway.

Student 1: You know that fellow, Soutar. I suspect he's a socialist. I overheard him making an impromptu speech to some friends of his about social injustice and all that.

Student 2: And I heard his father's just a joiner!

Student 1: With his own business though – a partnership!

Student 2: I don't know why they have to let these types into university. Entirely the wrong class! They just stir up trouble! *(they exit)*

Soutar A: Did she say 'stir up trouble? *(laughs)* I was quite guid at that! I hatit Anglo-Saxon and instead of grittin ma teeth an accepting it, I led a revolution of one, taking on the university establishment wi a crass bravado that was joyous to behold.

Enter Soutar B and Finlayson

Soutar B: Oh Finnel! I've been slaving away at Anglo-Saxon for weeks now and it's driving me mad! I should be reading poetry – writing poetry. Anything's better than this useless rubbish.

Finalyson: That's academe for you! At least at Art College they mak us paint! *We* dinna spend hoors porin ower critical academic work.

Soutar B: I envy you. Listen, Finnel, it's time someone spak oot aboot this hingover frae mediaeval days.

Finlayson: Whit can ye dae? It's in the course, so that's that.

Soutar B: No. If you don't like a thing, change it. My campaign is already far advanced. I've written an article for *The Student*. Revolution is what we need.

Finlayson: Ye'll only get intae trouble!

Soutar B: Hang that. Do you think I spent two years in the navy to worry about a few mangy old professors! *(he produces a paper)* Here – read this.

Finlayson: "What of Anglo Saxon"... *(to Soutar)* You dinna mince yer words.

Soutar B: *(impatiently)* Go on man! Read it!

Finlayson: "The study of Anglo Saxon may offer valuable background to the intending specialist. But to the ordinary student with a prospective career in teaching or journalism, it is largely redundant." – Strong stuff, old boy.

Soutar B: *(snatching the paper back)* There's more. "Anglo-Saxon occupies too much time, hours which should be given to more significant study of great masters of English are dragged into slave labour..."

Finlayson: Weill, and what did the old Professor hae tae say aboot yer campaign?

Soutar B: *(chuckling)* Not a bloody word. But the rest o the students in Honours English are fair delighted wi it! I'm a hero!

Finlayson: Ay, but when it comes tae the bit, no yin o them'll back ye up.

Soutar B: *(ignoring this)* I was narked though that Prof. Grierson didnae even look in my direction.

Finlayson: Lucky you. I hope ye left it at that?

Soutar B: No chance. I wrote Grierson direct, repeating what I'd said. The bugger paid no attention tae ma first letter, so I wrote him again demanding an interview!

Finlayson: Are you tryin tae get expelled? I also saw yer piece in *The Student*, satirising the professorial style!

Soutar B: *(with some glee)* Yin o ma better pieces, I thought! *(he declaims the following)*

> Here, from my chair, I desquamate my thought
> Like some strange snake in ecolysis;
> Shedding my cloak of knowledge every day.
> Like some bald, brindled bastard of a bird...

Finlayson: *(laughing)* Well, Joan of Arc, Jesus Christ, or whoever the hell ye think ye are... dinnae come rinnin tae me...

Lights down and up again. Soutar B strides into a room where Professor Grierson is sitting at a desk. Grierson is perusing a slim volume of poems. It is Gleanings, *Soutar's first book. Soutar coughs politely.*

Soutar B: You asked tae see me, Sir.

Grierson: Yes, Soutar. Your results in the Shakespeare exam were – hmm – pretty dud, I would say.

Soutar B: Yes, sir.

Grierson: I remember the last time I saw you – at your own insistence. You had rather a lot to say for yourself.

Soutar B: About Anglo-Saxon. Yes, I made my view quite plain. To my mind the study ought to be purely voluntary. It is no use to me.

Grierson: I thought I dealt very generously with you. While I refused to implement your suggestion as a matter of departmental policy, I turned a blind eye to your non-attendance at classes – (giving your attentions to the billiard hall, I believe) – and I bent the rules to allow you to sit Honours nonetheless.

Soutar B: That is true, sir. Your treatment of me was undoubtedly fair.

Grierson: But I did assume that you would apply yourself diligently to the studies of the "Great Masters of English literature" – once you had been freed from the "slave labour" of Anglo Saxon. *(he waves Soutar's book)* I see you are more interested in immortality for yourself.

Soutar B: What's literature worth if it's not living in the present.

Grierson: I'm not sure if these verses achieve that ambition. Strikes me as a lot of derivative, romantic pastiche!

Soutar B: Some critics would disagree with you, Sir. *Gleanings – by an Undergraduate* has got very good reviews for a first book.

Grierson: No doubt! No doubt your devotion to the Poetic Muse has led you to ignore totally that large area of literature commonly known as 'fiction'. You don't seem to have read any of the prescribed novels – apart from – I hazard a guess, the first hundred pages of *Tom Jones*.

Soutar B: I'm not interested in the novel, Sir. It's a decadent and bourgeois art form.

Grierson: *(stifling his annoyance)* At this late stage, so soon before your finals, I must warn you that you may be gleaning from life as an undergraduate for the rest of your life.

Soutar B: Yes, Sir.

Grierson: And I would say this. You have made a considerable nuisance of yourself during your four years here, and have been treated with some tolerance and understanding. But the Honours course is an opportunity for specialist study, for those who are maturely committed to the subject. It is not designed to meet the needs of – hmm – Minor Poets, Geniuses, or Journalists! These should roam thr' the curricula – at large. M'Yes! Good-day, Soutar.

Grierson exits. Soutars A and B stroll round the stage, as if walking down a street, talking to each other.

Soutar A: He wisnae bein totally unfair, old Grierson. He had introduced me to Donne – for which I wis grateful. And he wis exactly right about hou much fiction I'd read! I was damned lucky, really, tae get a Third Class Honours degree – I'm not a 'Varsity bird' *(he brushes his sleeve)* – one is apt tae get cobwebs on one's wings.

Soutar B: Yes – *(he is quoting from his own verse)* There I walked with stiffening bones Among the academic stones...

Soutar A: Professor Fraser's final diagnosis: "extreme osteoarthritis of the spine. Various suggestions o treatment were made, includin light spinal massage, intestinal antiseptics and the use of a vaccine prepared from the stools." Ugh!

Soutar B: Hmm – well, the first time ma feet gied me trouble wis at the end o the war – about a month after I had that food poisoning – I wonder if that did for me? The treatment sounds awful, mair like a full-time job.

And I'm getting stiffer as years go by – I'm 25 now – what'll I be like when I'm thirty... *(he stops abruptly, as if reluctant to answer his own question)* Ach, weill, pip-pip. Back to Perth and the folks. Nae mair Moray House – tedious teacher training. And nae mair thinkin o journalism – the *Scotsman* didn't want me anyway...

Soutar A: So take your last walk alang Princes Street, through the gairdens. Stroll alang Shandwick Place – Wait! Stop here at St. George's wi its Corinthian pillars! Here, boy, here – you've a decision tae make! *(he waves his hand like a wand)*

He stops under the pillars of St. George's West in Edinburgh. He puts up his hand, touches the stone, feels it thoughtfully.

Soutar A: ... Now you can be a poet...

Soutar B: ...Now I can be a Poet!

Act 1 Scene 4

Gauze Fly in room during poems. Enter Children

This poetic interlude should be done in slightly surreal manner, since it is out of the future rather than the present. At this time in Soutar's career, he is not writing anything like this. There should be a general air of prophecy.

Child: Wintry Nicht

Whit dae ye think I saw last nicht
Whan the mune cam owre Kinnoull
A puddock, wi' a cannel-licht,
Wha socht his puddock-stool.

The wintry wind gluff'd oot his glim
And skirl'd ahint a sauch
The chitterin' schedows loup at him;
The mune shog'd wi a lauch.

Doun be a dyke he grat alane;
Puir beast, sae made a mock:
The frostit draps dirl'd ane by ane
Upon the frostit rock.

Child: The Daft Tree

> A tree's a leerie kind o loon,
> Weel happit in his emerant goun
> Through the saft, simmer days:
> But, fegs, whan baes are in the fauld
> And birds are chitterin wi' the cauld,
> He coosts aff a' his claes

Child: The Lanely Mune

> Saftly, saftly, through the mirk
> The mune walks a' hersel:
> Ayont the brae, abune the kirk;
> And owre the dunnlin bell.
> I wadna be the mune at nicht
> For a' her gowd and a' her licht. *(Exit children)*

Fly gauze, revealing the wooden panelled room of 27 Wilson Street. Enter John and Margaret Soutar, leading Soutar B behind them. John Soutar makes a guesture of welcome.

John Soutar: Here it is! Finished! Mums, welcome tae yer new hame!

Margaret: Och, John, it's real bonnie! Whit a job ye've made o it. Look at the panelling! That's no juist joinery – it's a work o art!

John: It's oor wee castle, 27 Wilson Street. *(turning to Margaret and holding her by both arms)* And ye're the queen o't.

Margaret: Awa wi ye, ye're gien me a reid face, so ye are!

John: Willie, you're the word-smith. Whit name have ye decided on fur oor hoose?

Soutar B: 'Ingle Neuk' is owre common, but 'ingle' is the hearth, eftir aa, an I thocht that 'lowe' has the richt glow, so hou aboot 'Inglelowe', for the fire an the licht at the hert o the hoose.

John: 'Inglelowe' it is then, Willie. I've put aa ma skill as a jiner intae makkin this the hoose o oor dreams!

Willie: And ye've succeeded! Soutar & MacQueen, quality carpenters, comes up trumps again! The hoose is magnificent! Whit a grand view o the gairden!

John: Ay, and it looks oot yonder tae Craigie Hill. Ye can sit and watch the seasons pass, even if ye cannae gang ootside yersel.

(realising he has said something tactless, he adds hastily) An the birdies hoppin in and oot o yon auld tree there.

Margaret: And there's space for shelves to haud yer books. Oor hoose gets mair like the Sandeman Library every day! Whit a range o books – Anatole France, Henry James, Chekhov, Maeterlink, Lawrence, Trotsky – and yer pal, MacDiarmid.

Willie: I wish I cud hae duin mair tae help ye, Faither! But at the jinery work I'm no even an amateur. You're the professional! The craftsman! An I've felt like Diogenes in his barrel durin the flittin, watchin' aab'dy else humpin furniture while I staun an loaf aroond.

John: Ye've duin whit ye culd. An ye've gien it a guid name. I hope we'll aa be happy here – as happy as God lets us be. *(Exit John and Margaret Soutar)*

Soutar A: So the world shrinks. As time goes by I can do less and less. Walking is an effort. Ony movement maun be considered, planned in advance. But I tend the garden, lay paths, plant flowers – potter about ... By the way, I discovered that Burns used 'Inglelowe' in yin o his poems. Damn't – there's naethin new under the sun! Ah well, the tradition – if unknown – is nevertheless illustrious!

The following poems are to be read by various readers.

Summer Song

Nae wind comes owre sae free
Upon the yirden rose –
As hill-blawn winds that gae
Whaur the white bloom grows.

There is nae biggit bower
Sae gledsome for the sicht
As the sma' wilder'd fleur
Flanterin wi' licht.

And herts will tine their fear
Whan love sae freely blaws,
Open to joy and care
As the sma', white rose.

The Earth Hings Like a Keekin'-Glass.

The earth hings like a keekin'-glass,
Upon the wa' o' nicht,
And there the sin wud see himsel'
Stude up in his ain licht.

Outby the levin's langest loup
The earth's sma' kinkles rin
But wha is yon that sklents attour
The shuther o' the sin?

Preface to Poems

Here are leaves in a heap
That arena dead, but sleep.

Bring the licht o' your e'en
And they will sune grow green

Lat you live breath gang owre
And their freshness will fleur

Gie the warmth o' your bluid
And you'll walk in a blythe wud.

Soutar B: But it gies me time tae watch and listen. Today, I watched a midgie die. The death scene was vigorous, the midge whirling round on the window sill as if pirouetting on its head. Suddenly it collapsed – dead – like a star going super-nova! O! To have that intensity in life!

Enter David Low, Soutar's friend from university days.

Soutar B: Hello David, full grown quack at last! Faither was tellin me you're assistant to Dr. Bisset, no less. How does it feel to hae carte blanch to kill folk ootright?

David Low: It gives me a real thrill, after all those years of university and training. You're to be my first guinea-pig!

Soutar B: I suppose you've come tae gie me ma injection. This is the fiftieth since I cam hame, twa years syne? I think we should celebrate! Nou see an dae it richt!

David: You can rely on me, Willie. I promise to give over only when I've got you writhing and screaming with pain.

Soutar B: That's ma man! Ye ken, whit bothers me is that they winna tell me onything. I get the massage an the injections, and

I'm supposed to believe they micht cure me. I've had consultations with Fraser and he tells me naethin. I've written tae Bisset insisting on a straight answer – but no a word frae him so far.

David: I know about your letter. And I've got Dr. Bisset's reply here. I said I would give it to you. *(hands over a letter)*

Soutar B: Let's ken the worst. *(reads)* "Your illness is due to a form of spondylitis caused by streptococci in the bowel, probably the result of food-poisoning at one time, resulting in concretion between vertebrae caused by rheumatoid arthritis." *(to Low)* Been too damned long in seeing about it, I suppose.

David: If your condition had been dignosed four or five years ago, something might have been done – but now ...

Soutar B: It's too late?

David: Yes.

Soutar B: So there's no hope of any improvement in the condition?

David: I'm afraid not.

Soutar B: And will I end up stiff as a poker? *(David Low is lost for words)* Confined to bed?

David: Willie – I ... *(he falters, not knowing what to say. Soutar sees he is upset, and swiftly interjects)*

Soutar B: I suppose I'd better mak the maist o my pins while I can. But a poet needs his arms and mind more than his legs! Even if I'm rigid as a ramrod I can still think. I'll be able to write and read?

David: I should think so.

Soutar B: Thank God for that! It's a relief to *know*. To have the truth at last! Now, let's hae that celebration! When I kent it was you that was coming, I asked Mums to lay in a few bottles o stout! Here's to the next 50 injections! *(puts his arm round David and leads him offstage)* If it disnae dae me ony guid, it'll no dae me ony hairm – eh, Davy boy!

Gauze: Suggestion of a lush June evening, bird-song, sound of a stream afar off, the sky darkening from deep blue to black as they walk.

Soutar B: Finnel, I never tire of this view frae Callerfountain. Look at Perth doun there – and the hills aa roond aboot, the cleuch o Kinnoull an the Tay sweepin round Moncrieffe Island and doun tae the sea. There's a sense o something underneath, a misty potential that you're aware o even if it's invisible.

Finlayson: I ken whit you mean: sometimes you might not know the pot's on the stove, but you can see the steam rising from it.

Soutar B: Right, old man. Perth – doun in the valley: it sucks in the rich vapours o the earth and hills. The winding Tay gaithers them ower its hundred and twenty miles and brings them doon here. And in simmer the delicious savour o this place maks the heart ache.

Finlayson: Ay, and in winter the cauld rime maks yer lungs feel as if they're fou o shards o broken gless!

Soutar B: Touché, Finnel. I'm waxing poetical. But up here ye feel suspended in time, ayont aathing. On ma wey up, I saw this bonnie lass on the swings. Completely caught up she was in swinging backwards and forwards, up and down ...

Finlayson: A human pendulum!

Soutar B: When ye see youth so perfectly captured in an instant – it seems a tragedy that she should ever change. Whit a tyrant time is!

Finlayson: Your lyricism is infectious. I feel it growing like moss out of my ears! *(deliberately pretentious)* Day and day and day I rot into potential accomplishment. Only by laborious weaving, strand by strand, can man shape the ladder by which he climbs to the stars!

Soutar B: And with your cynicism chilling my soul like your Perth rime, I ask – Who's gonnae fix the damned ladder?!

Finlayson: Maybe it's a matter of geography. We're too far north here to be worshippers of Astarte.

Soutar B: Instead of aspiring to the stars, we are trapped in the glaur.

Finlayson: ... Looking at the worms!

Soutar B: Ay, the northern Muse is nippy like the frost!

Finlayson: And bitter like the hoary rime o Perth! *(Finlayson exits. Soutar A comes forward to the audience)*

Soutar A: The air's vibrant here. The lushness of Perthshire speaks to you, saying life is good, enjoy it while you can. It's a magical place, with a haunting sense of history, of the past in the present and the present in the past. Even in the hert o the toun, the river coursed through. And all those distant skylines. These hills speak to me in a quiet voice that I feel deep within ...like a gowk calling in the far-off wuid..

Reader: in a voice which is loud but not raucous - slightly haunting

> Hauf doun the hill, whaur fa's the linn
> Far frae the flaught o' fowk,
> I saw upon a lanely whin
> A lanely singin' gowk:
> *Cuckoo, Cuckoo,*
> And at my back
> The howie hill stude up and spak:
> *Cuckoo, Cuckoo.*
>
> There was nae soun': the loupin linn
> Hung frostit in its fa'
> Nae bird was on the lanely whin
> Sae white wi' fleurs o snaw:
> *Cuckoo, Cuckoo,*
> I stude stane still;
> And saftly spak the howie hill:
> *Cuckoo, Cuckoo.*

Fade to Black

Act 1 Scene 5

Soutar B: That bugger Christopher Grieve – Hugh MacDiarmid – poet extraordinaire! Four letters I wrote him in four months – and not a whisper of a reply. Let's see if this'll raise him... "Dear Chris, – Tick off your best excuse and sign..." *(after most of these 'items', Soutar adds a satirical aside)*

1. I am dead (I hope not – really I do...)
2. I am fed up (Of course he is – Scotland's not a good place for any poet to be)
3. I am on a world tour (geographical area in line with literary ambitions!)

4. I am Labour candidate for Pango – but am still looking for it (His political notions are so extreme that only somewhere obscure would have him.)

5. I am at Missolonghi writing a sonnet sequence on Byron. Greeks daily supply me with Samian wine. Have dashed down a goodly number of cups. Byron advised it (Any chance fur a dram!)

6. I am reading ma poems o genius in October chapbook" (Damned good – even if he says so himself!)

7. I am at 10 Downing Street at present prospective successor to the PM (Whaur's yer Ramsay MacDonald noo? At least Grieve's a socialist and a Scotsman.)

MacDiarmid: Sorry I've been such a bad correspondent lately.

Soutar B: *(warmly)* Forget it, Christopher – but why have you kept your head down for so long?

MacDiarmid: I've been expanding my ideas about a Scottish renaissance in poetry and the arts.

Soutar B: Just like that, eh?

MacDiarmid: I noticed that you didn't have a poem in Munro's varsity anthology? Mind you it was so unalleviatedly pedestrian that you couldn't possibly have been in it.

S outar B: I aye felt out of place at university, even among those who were interested in poetry. So I wisnae surprised that none of my stuff was in. The worst review my book *Gleanings* got was from *The Student* magazine!

MacDiarmid: For too long literature in Scotland has been deaved by alien – and inferior – models from England. English poetry is moribund – its head buried in sands of past magnificence. Where are the interesting poets springing up? Ireland: Yeats – America: Pound and Eliot – and I hear stirrings in Wales too – and *(he preens himself)* of course here in Scotland.

Soutar B: I hope I can contribute here and there.

MacDiarmid: Of course. Even those early poems of yours catapulted you into the company of the few in Scotland whose verse is worth a damn.

Soutar B: Oh, I liked *Sangschaw*!

MacDiarmid: My new book!

Soutar B: But why on earth are you writing in Scots, Chris? Two years ago, you were raging about Scots being a language fit only for sentimental idiots, old grannies and ladies' knitting circles – or stage Scoats Coamics!

MacDiarmid: Well, so it was until I resurrected it.

Soutar B: I can see you changed your mind. To take up Scots as an occasional matter is one thing, but to use it solidly throughout a whole collection is another.

MacDiarmid: The problem with Scots is the vocabulary we've lost to English. If Scots is to be more than a language of couthy sentiment – and I think we agree that's not enough – it must have the status of a literary language, and be able to speak to the world at large. So we must go to the dictionary, and relearn the language we have lost to English linguistic empire-building. I've already done it: sat down with Jamieson's dictionary to memorise the vocabulary, beginning with the letter 'A' – and by the time I got to 'C' – I was writing great poetry! – 'The Bonnie Broukit Bairn'

> Mars is braw in crammasy,
> Venus in a green silk goun,
> The auld muin shak's her gowden feathers,
> Their starry talk's a wheen o blethers,
> Nane for thee a thochtie sparin',
> Earth, thou bonnie broukit bairn!
> – *But greet, an' in yer tears, ye'll droun*
> *The hale clanjamfrie!*

Soutar B: *(after a pause)* That's very fine. And it fits your programme by using Scots to convey ideas...

MacDiarmid: Quite so, Soutar, quite so.

Soutar B: But I still maintain that the big things will have to be done in English, which has a genuinely international audience.

MacDiarmid: *(visibly annoyed)* Nonsense: English is like the race that use it – dead from the neck up, compromising dodos, parading their stuffed shirts round a contracting empire which is just about to wake up and sling them out.

Soutar B: *(determined not to be overawed by the older man)* I respect what you are doing, Chris, but don't you think you're making too much of it.

MacDiarmid: I've hardly started. My new work is an epic called *'A Drunk Man Looks at the Thistle'*. With this single poem, I bring Scottish literature firmly into the forefront of the European modernist tradition. "A Scottish poet maun assume/The burden o' his people's doom/And dee to brak' their livin' tomb". *(he says this to Soutar – both of course unaware of the irony)* My poem will transform literature in Scotland.

Soutar B: Let's hope it will – but you're setting up a programme which even you can't live up to. Now, my notion is to write for the bairns, to involve them in relishing Scots as a language – I've made yin or twa sallies into this area – using a fairly dense register of Scots. *("Cock Craw"):*

Soutar A: Fu' heich upon the midden-cairn
It is his cronie chanticleer
Wha blaws the bugill o' the bairn
To lat the hale world ken he's here.
Liggan sae comfy wi' the kye
And a muckle eerie licht outby
He's wauken'd up the ox and craw...

MacDiarmid: Do I detect an influence from *Sangschaw*, perhaps? But your use of Scots is natural and sound. You have a genuine ear for it.

Soutar B: I admit that your Scots lyrics did inspire me to try my hand at oor ain leid. But my point is that you hae tae bring in the bairns if the language is to live on.

MacDiarmid: That's the wrong end of the horse! We need a literature for adult minds, not for children or adolescents. If great poetry is written in any language it doesn't matter a hoot if nobody can read it but the man who wrote it. I don't think the artist should be concerned with his audience or that art subserves any purpose except its own development. Now, I'm not likely to be the man to write these bairn-rhymes or repopularise Scots. It's enough for me that *I* use the language.

Soutar B: I can't be as dogmatic as you are, but we're on the same track and micht meet somewhaur in the middle. But I'm no tae adopt your manifesto juist because you assert it.

MacDiarmid: I like a man with a mind of his own – though it's a pity so many condemn themselves to be wrong by holding a different opinion to myself – I suppose that's life.

Soutar B: *(rising)* Well, I don't often get the chance to have such good 'jaws' about poetry with people in Perth.

MacDiarmid: Men of my own calibre are indeed exceedingly rare.

Soutar B: *(laughing)* I've a healthy conceit of my own abilities too!

MacDiarmid: Take care of yoursel, man. Scotland needs her poets. *(Lights fade. Exit Soutar and MacDiarmid)*

Soutar A: Then lively, laughing, mischievous Evelyn came into our lives:

(Soutar A in spot. John and Margaret talking to Soutar A)

John Soutar: We've news for ye, Willie. While you were away at Montrose, yer Auntie Beenie cam up tae see us wi a proposeetion. Ye ken the folks in Australia young Evelyn, yer distant cousin. Mind her faither Alec wis killed bi a shark a year syne.

Soutar A: Ay – a nesty wey to go. An' her mither wis killed in a motor accident no lang efter.

Margaret S: Nae wee lass o six year auld shuld be left athoot a mither and faither.

John Soutar: We aye hoped that a brither or sister wud come alang tae be company tae ye.

Soutar A: I'd a liked a brither – an' mair nor that a wee sister – but insteid I've hud ye baith ae masel!

Margaret S: Beenie suggestit that Evelyn shuld come here tae live an' we should adopt her.

Soutar A: That's a fine thocht. But will ye cope wi a lively six-year-auld?

John Soutar: I'm no sayin it'll be easy. We're gettin a bit lang in the tooth, but a young lassie aboot the hoose'll keep us young. And ye can help tae bridge the generation gap.

Soutar A: *(trying to make it easier for his parents, not putting obstacles in their way)* Weill, as lang's she disna keep me aff my readin!

Margaret S: Huh! Yince ye get yer heid in a book the warld could gae up in smoke an ye'd no notice!

Soutar A: Evelyn's welcome here if ye ask me. It'll be guid for us aa. Noo sit ye doon noo and write tae Beenie. Say we're aa pleased that Evelyn comes tae bide wi's.

Margaret S: It's time for oor daily worship.

John Soutar: *(his language slightly more anglicised than normal)* We thank the Lord for the joy o bein thegither in this fine hoose, wi aa the comforts we could want, in the middle o the loveliest kintraside in Scotland. We pray the Lord to guide us in bringing Evelyn intae oor home, to show us how tae raise her in the nurture and admonition o the Lord. Help us tae gie her aa that she needs. *(the rest a murmur)* ...Amen. *(exit John and Margaret).*

Soutar B sits down at a table burdened with large tomes and makes several attempts at writing. The lighting is subdued.

Company: *(loud) Epitaph on a Potential Poet who Learned the Meaning of Every Word in the English Dictionary*

> Ten years he labour'd till his mind was stor'd;
> Then turn'd to greet experience with a word:
> But, ere his hand had written half a whit,
> He met a truth and left no word of it.

Silence. Soutar B throws down his pen in disgust

Soutar A: *(with the knowledge of hindsight and an air of mischief)*

> The Yager (the horsed devil)
>
> As abalone glows with nacre
> Thus glows he when the roaring saker
> Showers in largesse, bruit on bruit
> Its fulgerant and baccate fruit.

Soutar B: Swallowing the dictionary's an adventure when ye try it. A poet's got to have a decent 'word hoard'. Because poets are like seers, prophets, we try tae see intae the hert and mind o God himsel, capturing the living quality in all things. Poetry is the greatest challenge, and I work hard at my apprenticeship ...I feel I'm on the right track – but at the moment, there's something missing... *(he looks to Soutar A, shrugs)*

Soutar A, like a magician, waves a wand. Enter Evelyn, a girl of 6, big, forward, determined, with Australian accent. They are working in the garden.

Evelyn: I like this house – there's lots of rooms in it for playing hide and seek. And my bedroom's nice – it stays in the one place. It doesn't go up and down like the ship...

Soutar B: Puir thing – that was a gey lang voyage for a wee lass like you. Did ye get lonesome?

Evelyn: Just a bit, at first. I got scared when I couldn't see land any more and it was just sea everywhere, for miles and miles. Every night I asked God to bring the land back, but in the morning there was just more and more sea.

Soutar B: Did the people on board ship look efter ye? Did ye hae ony wee girls yer ain age tae pley wi?

Evelyn: It was dinkum. I had more people to play with than I've ever had before – and I made a special friend – Susan. *(she is energetically pulling up weeds)* Look Willie, there's a little weed. Shall I pull it out?

Soutar B: Evelyn, leave that alane. Yon's no a weed – it's my prize pansy.

Evelyn: *(dancing with mischief and ignoring every word he's said)* Look at this big blue weed *(she has a gladioli in her hand)* I've pulled it up for you!

Soutar B: Ma best gladioli! *(Soutar holds his back, he winces with pain).*

Evelyn: What's the matter? Are you sore? I'll give you my big weed to make you better.

Soutar B: I've got a stiff back, Evie. I've got to watch how I move. *(he kneels down rigidly)* Now look here, wee one. You don't pull anything up unless I tell you. Understand.

Evelyn: *(a bit weepy)* But I was only trying to help you...

Soutar B: I *know*... Don't cry – here, listen to this wee rhyme I've made up for you.

Evelyn: What's a rhyme?

Soutar B: A poem. Like a song, except there isn't any music.

Evelyn: You made it up for me? When did you do that? I only got here yesterday!

Soutar B: I made it up right here, watching you destroy my garden!

Evelyn: *(wailing)* I didn't mean it, honest!

Soutar B: Sshh. Listen. *(he points to the appropriate part of Eve as he recites the poem)*

> How would you believe
> That a little lass, Eve
> Has a foot to each boot
> And an arm in each sleeve.

Evelyn: I do have a foot to each boot, and an arm in each sleeve. But that's silly – I've always known that!

Soutar B: So you didn't like my wee rhyme! *(in a feigned huff)* Well, I won't make up any more for you.

Evelyn: Oh I'm sorry. I did like your poem, honest. And I like it because you made it special for me.

Soutar B: I don't believe you.

Evelyn: But I do like it. I do! I do! Willie, please promise you'll write lots of poems, lots and lots, just for me!

Soutar B: *(laughing)* I promise I'll make up lots and lots of poems.

Evelyn: Lots and lots of poems, just for me.

Soutar B: Now, come and help me dig some holes here to plant my lettuces.

Evelyn is paying no attention, but has started to dig furiously in the green. Soutar has been absorbed in his work. Suddenly he notices what she's doing.

Soutar B: You little minx. Look at the hole you've made in my green!

Evelyn: I was trying to make it go up and down like the sea!

Soutar B: I think you need another wee poem:

Evelyn: What's this one called? You didn't give the last one a name.

Soutar B: *(kneels down in front of her)* I'll call it 'Do not jump too hard on my be-double-u-tiful green':

> It is horrid to be seen
> Making holes upon my green
> You might jump upon a snail
> Or stamp on a beetle's tail
> And how sad it is, alas!
> When you break a blade of grass
> If you sit upon a spider
> You will see what is inside her!
> O! be careful, tippy toe,
> When across my green you go ...

Evelyn: I'll be careful, tippy toe,
When across your green I go...

He lifts her up with obvious difficulty.

Soutar B: Right, my lollipop. Let's see how my sweet peas are doing... Just look at this flourish of flooers, bonnie, isn't it...
(exit Soutar B and Evelyn)

Soutar A: Evie changed my life. She was the sister I never had – and the daughter I'd never have. And as my bones grew stiffer, she could move. She kept my childhood alive – and my manhood too. I loved her mischief, her nonsense.

Those last years o freedom, until 1929, were precious. I could still go oot to parties, have fun, flirt wi the girls. I'd dance the hours awa and carouse deep intae the nicht, singing, dancing, cracking jokes – my wit sparkled mair as the nicht went on. But I cursed this dud back o mine. How I longed juist for yin night to fling myself into the fun as I uised tae. Fun isnae fun if you dinna get intae hells bells. And I cut quite a dashing figure...

In Edinburgh, there were several women in love wi me, wrote me admiring letters, protestations of liking, even of love. I was a mad and fickle flirt. But nane of them attracted me with anything stronger than an animal sexuality. They gave me affection, and mair... and all I did was dally wi them. And there wis yin woman... Eventually, guilt began to strike:

Soutar B: I send my words; they are a song
Though sorrowful their token;
I send my words; to you belong
Words never spoken.
There was a death – whose ghost is shame
Until the living –
When you gave love and I became
Less worthy by the giving.

Soutar A: No woman caught my imagination more than Daisy, dear Daisy in mourning – Daisy o the auld days o Perth Academy.

Reader: As snug beside my jo I lay
I dreamt my auld jo cam tae me,
Her deid cheeks white like leprosy
As snug beside my jo I lay
She leugh'd and sklented owre the strae
Her cauld lips roun' for me tae pree –
As snug beside my jo I lay
I dreamt my auld jo cam tae me.

Soutar A: I kent that in real life I wisnae much o a prospect for a woman – no job – health dicey, the ever stiffening corp. I wis liability enough tae my parents, how could I dae that tae a swack young lassie. That didnae stop me actin the sheik with ony attractive wench that cam ma way, but that's as far as it went. And, oh, how I longed for a woman who might push aside my illness and reach out to me... But you cannot censor the language of dreams. There my thwarted sexuality showed itsel in full, throbbing colours...

Dream Sequence – almost harem like. Loud late twenties dance music. Soutar B comes on with a "light fluffy thing" – a young woman who is obviously not averse to advances being made to her. They begin a dance which becomes quickly more and more passionate. Soutar becomes more and more aroused, until he grabs hold of her in a licentious embrace, and says, almost cave-man like "Gimme a kiss!" As they kiss, another woman enters, wearing a long, dark cloak. As the embrace comes to an end, Soutar looks up at the other woman, who throws open her cloak to reveal that she is wearing only little bathing pants. Blackout. Exit the two girls. Enter a woman dressed in Eastern fashion, coming downstage as if in a trance, with wide open but expressionless eyes. As she approaches Soutar, she stumbles, and nearly falls, but Soutar springs up and catches her. When she regains ballance, Soutar deliberately secures his grip round her waist. She turns towards him slowly, and responds to his embrace. Then starts to lead him off. Meanwhile Soutar A lies down, as if to sleep, and murmurs the following, voicing Soutar B's thoughts:

Soutar A: You want me to come with you? All right, I'm coming. What? Down this narrow wynd? But it's so dank and dark. Where now? Round this bend? Up this close? What are you doing to me?

Voice: You are to ascend to 'Queen of the Castle'. You must be prepared.

Soutar A: Who the devil is that?

Voice: The Queen arouses the passion of a man and then becomes cold and bitter towards him – that is her form of torture...

Soutar B is spinning round on stage, gradually resuming normal movement and mood.

A woman in bridal dress is glimpsed at the back of the stage. Soutar B goes to her side, and she takes his arm. A disembodied voice intones...

Voice: ...I now pronounce you man and wife. You may kiss the bride.

Soutar B moves to kiss her, but she collapses in his arms. He picks her up and carries her in his arms to the front of the stage, and kneels down, cradling her in his arms.

Soutar A: My darling! What's wrong. *(he listens to her breathing)* No breath, not a movement. O... *(he holds her close, crooning sorrowfully to her. Suddenly she revives)*

Girl: *(speaking as if nothing had happened)* What a wonderful day it's been. But we must move on out of the church. The car, the photographer, they're waiting for us.

Soutar B: *(choking with emotion)* But my dear, you have been dead...

Girl: No, Willie, it's you who have been dead...

End of Act 1

Act II Scene 1

Soutar A: Any hopes I had were dashed by the decline in my health. In February 1929, I contracted pneumonia in my right lung – and a pain in my side Dr. Low diagnosed as pleurisy. Aa that summer, my right hip ached and my right leg seemed somehow longer than the left. Yin day in June, I was crippled by the pain in my groin – as if a vertebra did a side-step – *(he grimaces)* like an electric shock in the middle o my back. It brocht me aamost to my knees. Then the doctor diagnosed arthritis in the right hip. The cure – *(he snorts cynically)* tae lie up wi weights at my leg to reduce the muscle-spasm.

One morning in January it took me ten minutes to get my right sock on. And I cursed and swore and use mair foul language in those ten minutes than in ony ten weeks o my life until then. Sometimes we forget to laugh at ourselves – pain is humour's poison.

Life was closing in. I stopped writing poetry. I found myself in a mental waste-land, where there was not a breath of inspiration.

My last trip tae Edinburgh wis in May – a beautiful time o year. As I waited for ma operation, I felt nothing wad come o it. At the end o the month, I cam hame for guid – my last journey but one. After that, getting up was mair and mair difficult, and finally, on 17th July, I resigned masel tae a full time existence stretched out in bed. My only attempt to get up, wi much help, wis sic a Pilgrim's progress I was geynear seik. That painful apotheosis wis the last until auld Gabriel blew.

Soutar B: It wis 3rd November, 1930.

Soutar A: I wis 32 year auld.

Soutar B: But before aa that hit me, there was probably the most real romantic episode in my life. My little cousin Mollie who for years had been visiting us ilka summer had blossomed intae a bonnie young woman. She moved me more than any woman since Daisy, and became for me a symbol of youth. She embodied – for good – my last, and most poignant love.

Soutar A: We used to flirt and get into mischief. We had sic fun thegither, Mollie, my auld old school friend Bill, and his sister Jess. Then, I found out that Bill had more than a fancy for Mollie, and was begging her to go oot with him. I felt a strange sense of loss, a niggling jealousy, and wished in ma hert o herts that I could tak her awa frae him.

Enter Mollie. She and Soutar B catch hold of each other's hands.

Soutar B: Bill was telling me he's asked you to go to the theatre with him. Do you want to go?

Mollie: Well, it's just a friendly night out.

Soutar B: *(putting his arms round Mollie)* I wouldn't want Bill to take my favourite wee cousin away from me completely.

Mollie: Don't be silly! He's just a pal!

Soutar B: *(speaking out of order)* Maybe it's a pity we have to stay 'just cousins'...

Mollie makes to reply, but only manages a stifled exclamation

Soutar B: No – don't answer that. Don't say anything. I shouldn't have said that. That's just the way things are.

Mollie: Nobody could take me away from you, Willie. Not Bill, not anybody.

Soutar B: Ach, enough of this. Give me my goodnight kiss and hug! *(they embrace)* Now, goodnight! *(she goes out, with a distinct look of regret on her face, a look directly echoed on Soutar's face).*

Soutar A: The romance blossomed – but it took time. Mollie aye seemed cool wi him, but didnae repulse his attentions. I wasn't conscious of being jealous of him – though ma dreams made that quite clear. But I convinced masel that it was guid fun watching the burgeoning amour o a pal – and took a naughty delight in the fact that my arm had often been around his girl. After a few months, things seemed at a standstill...

Enter Bill.

Bill: Hello, Willie. Your mother let me in.

Soutar B: Come awa in. Guid tae see ye, man.

Bill: Willie, I want to speak to you.

Soutar B: Why of course, Bill. Fire away.

Bill: It's about Mollie. As you know, I've been seeing her as often as I can for months now. At first I thought I was getting somewhere. She seemed to like my company – pleased to see me.

Soutar B: Well?

Bill: You know I got a surveying job down in Sutton near where Mollie stays?

Soutar B: Of course, Bill – I didn't think that it was a coincidence.

Bill: It wasn't. I really thought that from there on it would just be a matter of time, seeing each other so regularly...

Soutar B: She'd be eating out of your hand in no time.

Bill: She's not eating out of my hand at all. She seems to like me a lot less than she did that night I took her out to the theatre – Boxing Day last year! You remember!

Soutar B: So what's happened?

Bill: There's nothing new – it's just that...

Soutar B: Come to the point, Bill...

Bill: There seems to be someone else on the horizon?

Soutar B: Someone else? Who?

Bill: Yoursel, Willie!

SoutarB: Me! Och, nonsense Bill!

Bill: It's true. God knows, I wish it wisnae. When I saw her last, I tried to push her to say what was the matter, and she blurted out that she couldn't fix on me when there was you...

Soutar B: She said that?

Bill: She did.

Soutar B: Well, you know, we've always been fond of each other – and I did have a pang o jealousy when you first asked her to go out with you. My health makes me a puir marriage prospect...

Bill: Nonsense – you're attractive to women – you ken that.

Soutar B: I admit that I've flirted with Mollie – before you declared you interest – but it was understood that it would never go beyond that...

Bill: For her, anyway, it seems to go a good deal beyond that.

Soutar B: Are you sure?

Bill: She told me – in not so many words. And now she feels she's treated me badly.

Soutar B: And how do you feel about her?

Bill: I want to marry her!

Soutar B: Bill, as far as I'm concerned, the relationship between

Mollie and me steys the same as ever it wis...

Bill: What shall I do?

Soutar B: Hang on. Be around – be patient – if you love her. She'll make up her mind in her ain time.

Bill: Will you speak to her? Well, anyway, she wants to speak to you.

Soutar B: So I'm to be the arbiter of souls! Phow! I wear no wig and never shall, but I'll speak to her anyway.

Later that same day, in front of gauze, Soutar and Mollie together, alone

Mollie: Don't think badly of me, Willie. I know Bill's one of your best friends – Now it's as if I've been leading him on, though I never meant to but I can't help how I feel.

Soutar B: *(taking her hand)* – Yes, Moll, the world is upside down, isn't it. But it's not for me, of all people, to judge you – or Bill.

Mollie: What should I do, Willie?

Soutar B: What your heart tells you to. But, Mollie, I'm no match for a woman – no salary – no prospects – a scribbler like me is never likely to earn mair nor a pittance – anyway, that's not the point. We've enjoyed each other's company, but we have tae keep it like that, haven't we.

Soutar is being just a bit sententious, Mollie is sensible of this, but her own feelings of guilt prevent her from fighting it.

Mollie: That's right, Willie.

Soutar B: Bill's very fond of you. – Moll, love's a tender plant, and it needs time and the right environment. If you have a little affection for Bill – say so – tell him – and tell me. *(a little honesty returns to the conversation here)* After all, you don't really know him yet. A blade is easily crushed – but a tree is a different matter.

They kiss and she goes off. As she approaches the wings, Bill, in the shadow, offers her his hand. She takes it and they exit.

Soutar B: *(aside)* Whit a nicht that wis – Mollie and I gabbed on until late – late, our feelings translated into elated conversation. But, puir Mollie – I must have hurt her feelings – shovelling them off onto someone else like that – even if it was Bill. I did want her – I was jealous – if I'd been honest, I would have told her that –

without arousing hopes I could never fulfil. But finally –
goodnight, Mollie – Bill's presence has never left the room
tonight.

Reader 1: He who weeps for beauty gone
Hangs about his neck a stone.

He who mourns for his lost youth
Daily digs a grave for truth.

He who prays for happy hours
Tramples upon earthy flowers.

He who asks an oath from love
Doth thereby his folly prove.

Mourn not overmuch, nor stress
After love or happiness.

He who weeps for beauty gone
Stoops to pluck a flower of stone.

pause

Reader 2: Out of the darkness of the womb
Into a bed, into a room:
Out of a garden into a town,
And to a country, and up and down
The earth; the touch of women and men
And back into a garden again:
Into a garden; into a room;
Into a bed and into a tomb;
And the darkness of the world's room.

Reader 3: Into the quiet of this room
Words from the clamorous world come:
The shadows of the gesturing year
Quicken upon the stillness here.

The wandering waters do not mock
The pool within its wall of rock
But turn their healing tides and come
Even as the day into this room.

Act II Scene 2

Soutar A: *(in bed)* Thirteen years... Thirteen years and four months in the same place. How mony people ken yin spot so well. Maybe the world is in a mess because it's aye in flux. Just when you think you have a picture or idea in view, it becomes false because reality has moved on. Maybe I've understood some things because I couldnae be pairt o the flux. Not having legs, my mind developed wings.

Whit difference would it have made gin I'd been fit in body these past six years? If my condition comes out of deep psychic necessity – and sometimes I wonder how it could be otherwise, surely the pain I have borne is naething if I've been able to write one good poem.

Soutar B: Do you remember the day I stopped at St. George's West Church in Edinburgh, put my hand on its grey sandstone pillar and murmured: 'Now I can be a poet'? Frae that day on I've been preparin masel for this vocation. Nou, here, in this little room in this little town, I am a poet. Nou the world staunds still for me, and as thirteen summers, fifty-three seasons circle roun, it is my thoughts and feelings, and my pen, that move. Time itsel, sometimes, seems to stop.

Soutar A: And so my life is writing a poem, ma diary, and ma journal for mair complex reflections. I feel even more the impulse to capture thoughts before they vanish like winnelstrae intae the air. And I record my dreams. For yin who'll never again enter a cinema door, dreams are a free, a nightly show, like spending a third of your life watching pantomime! And there are letters tae write, riddles, epigrams, rough jottings – an infinity o books tae read – I wonder I ever had time to walk around.

The warld comes to me instead: the visitors stream in and out: relations, neighbours, ministers, well-meaning 'sick visitors', sometimes even my friends. My parents look after my every need, and there's Eve, my wee butterfly sister, aye dancing to pastures new. That is my life.

And I finished ma long poem – 'The Auld Tree'. I want to prove the New Scots Dictionary isnae just a mortuary for Scots words, a literary orphanage. It maun be a foundation stone or it'll be a tombstone. "On this hard soil the seed of Scotland must either wither or bear fruit. Our language is the image of our soul – we maun possess our soul until we hae a living language."

Soutar B: *(in spotlight)*
> Ah shairly, gin nae makar's breath
> Blaw süne thru Scotland, doun to death
> She'll gang and canker a' the world.
> Owre lang her bastard sons hae skirl'd
> Around the reid rose; wha sall name
> The wild, sma' white-rose o' our hame...

Soutar A: Richt in the rowsan sin the wud
> O' great green tree sae leamin' stüde
> Like it had been a buss o' fire;
> And as it stude the warblin' choir
> O' birds were singin' o' their hame:
> But what they sang I canna name
> Though I was singin' wi' the birds
> In my ain countrie's lawland words.

Soutar B: I wauken'd; and my hert wis licht
> (Though owre my ain hill cam the nicht)
> For aye yon aintrin hill I saw
> Wi' its green tree in the gowdan daw:
> And, as I swaver'd doun the slack,
> I heard, aye branglant at my back,
> The challance o' the singin' word
> That whunners like a lowin' sword

Soutar A: "The challance o' the singin' word." A ringing line. I've dedicated the poem tae MacDiarmid, but he's no impressed!

MacDiarmid: *(in spot)* To have a poem dedicated to one doesn't mean one has to like it! I appreciate its merits, but my own practice of Scots is so individual and inimitable that it justifies in my case alone, I believe – so I'm the worst man to pass judgement. 'The Auld Tree' is cluttered up with unvivified, useless words ...I feel that regarding Scots I've been a thoroughly bad influence on you..." *(exit)*

Soutar A: I think it's a guid poem. But we all have our own forms of self-esteem and I've a tough shell around masel – so I scarcely feel a patronising pat. All honour to Grieve – but I am not his disciple and if I write in Scots, that disnae make me his protégé. Anyhow, what is language gin it isnae bearin a national utterance? If I belang tae onythin it is tae Scotland, and if I hae a talent, it is my parents'.

Soutar A in bed, Margaret bustling about him.

Margaret Soutar: *(tidying away the wash-basin).* Yer faither's comin up tae see ye in a minute.

Soutar A: That wee freend o Evelyn's, Ann, cam in wi Eve the ither day. Ye ken hou she's aye been a bittie shy wi me?

Margaret S: Ay, but bairns are aften strange wi a body that's in bed.

Soutar A: Weill, she comes in, her head cocked on yin side, luiked me up an' doun an says, "Willie, how many legs have you got?" So I tellt her I've got twa, but she shaks her heid an says, solemn as you like – "No – you've only got ONE".

Margaret S: Bairns say the queerest things. Juist like Evelyn.

Soutar A: Yes?

Margaret S: She wis askin if she'd had the measles – there's an ootbrak o them at the skule. I tellt her she probably had them a few years syne, and that you had them when ye were 18 months auld.

Soutar A: So ye say – I dinna mind it masel!

Margaret S: Lissen, will ye. Dae ye ken what the wee bissum said! She said, "Why did ye let him recover?"

Soutar A: *(mainly in jest, but with a touch of irony)* Good question!

Margaret S: Richt, that's you ready fur the day. *(she bangs into John Soutar coming into the room)* Whoops! John! Watch whaur yer gaun! *(she exits)*

John Soutar: Sorry, Mither! *(going to Soutar)* Michty me, ye're luikin gey braw in yer new gear! I've brocht ye yer poast. The usual clutch o letters. Noo, I'm awa doon the toun, so is there onythin ye want while I'm oot?

Soutar A: Could ye post these letters fur me? I'm needin paper an' stamps.

John Soutar: It wad be a tragedy, richt eneuch, gin ye were tae be athoot paper! An' ye'll be needin mair fags.

Soutar A: Ay, Dad, I'm smokin' bonny these days – I lie here, eatin, sleepin, readin and smokin 'bines! I luik the healthiest invalid in Perth. Whit a life, eh! *(with a touch of bitterness)* Whit luxury!

John Soutar: *(sitting with Soutar to relieve his mood)* By the way, I heard this story aboot this Perthshire worthy, Willie Pitcaithley, a builder chiel workin on this auld body's cottage. Noo, Willie had niver clappit een on corrugated iron afore, and when the gaffer gied him this stuff, an tellt him tae pit it on the ruif o the building, he said: "It'll be awfae stuff that, juist like a sclater's erse – owre cauld in winter an' owre het in simmer".

Soutar A: *(laughing)* I like that, Faither, here's yin for you: This woman, 'Mrs Broun o Spittalfield' wis returnin frae the Kirk yin Sabbath whan the rain cam doun. Wi a new hat on, and wi'oot an umbrella she liftit up her muckle skirt frae the back and tentit it owre her heid. But she'd liftit up her petticoat an aa an wis walkin alang, her lower body in full view. An elder catched her up an says, "Excuse me, Mrs Broun, but ye're exposin yer person". "Tuts!" says Mrs Broun. "Whit aboot ma person – it's fifty year auld – but this a new hat I hae on."

Och, Faither, there are three things I miss sorely: I'd gie onythin tae hae anither dander owre Callerfountain, and tae see anither Chaplin film – and I'd like, juist yince mair, to join in an eightsome reel...

Enter Eve like a mini-hurricane. She runs over to the bed and plants a noisy kiss on Soutar's face. He puts an arm around her.

Eve: Hello, Willie!

Soutar A: Hi ya, ma wee puddledoo!

Eve: Guess what I've found!

Soutar A: A frog!

Eve: No, but you're close. I've got it outside. *(to John Soutar)* Can I bring it in to show Willie?

John Soutar: I suppose that depends whit it is.

Eve runs out to fetch it.

John Soutar: *(to Soutar A)* I wonder whit the wee minx has in store for us.

Re-enter Eve.

Eve: Shut yer eyes and open yer hands!

Soutar A: Aa richt – ma een are ticht shut!

Eve: Open them now!

Soutar A: A hedgehog! I havnae seen yin o thaim for years. He seems quite joco. Look at his wee bricht een, Faither! *(he hands the hedgehog on to John Soutar, who, scratching and not pleased, takes it out)*

Eve: Do you think there's a story about him...

Soutar A: I'm shair there is, now let me see... *(lights fade on the scene, leaving Soutar and Eve deep in story-telling).*

Soutar B: Teeth-water at 6.45. Shaving gear. Fire lit: breakfast and newspaper: subscription to nature's 'pirlie-pig' collected: washing water: feet dusted and bed made: table and accessories lifted over: room dusted. Tea: 'water-works': wireless on for news: fire kept going: supper: wireless: table etc. lifted back: foot-pads shifted and bed clothes arranged: fire still burning brightly – until 11 or 11.30. And mair: like hair washing – sic a performance that the haill family foregaither for the spectacle – and extras like entertaining friends. An endless list – and this is what I daily take for granted.

Enter Eve – in adult persona.

Eve: And what did we get? Willie, always being there. Everything I did I brought to him: stories of school, the mischief I got up to, my singing, learning to cook and sew, the fun and games, balloon fights and pillow fights. He entertained all my friends. He gave me songs and stories, true ones, made up ones, bible games, and the practical jokes he played. And the bairn-rhymes he'd recite to me in the evening... there was so much we daily took for granted...

Soutar B: I didnae just scrieve the bairn-rhymes for Eve, although I couldna hae duin them athoot her. It was because I believed that gin my ain tongue, Scots, was tae hae a future it wad come on a cock-horse, on the tongues o the bairns...

There follows a sequence in which children, watched by the two Soutars and Eve, act out bairn-rhymes, complete with action. This sequence is non-naturalistic in style and method, resembling an interlude in a pantomime, using bright and changing lights, according to the poem.

Soutar A: *(as if an enticement into another world)*

Titles not to be spoken:

Come Awa

Come in tae the neuk;
Come awa, come awa;
It's whistlin' yowdendrift o!

The mune's gaen yont like a muckle heuk
Tae hairst the snaw fae the lift o!

Soutar B: Come in tae the lowe;
Come awa, come awa;
It blaws baith snell an' sair o!
Noo the onding's smoorin' hicht an' howe
An' the peesie wheeps nae mair o!

Children: *(four speaking, two skipping. These instructions may vary depending on the numbers of children, etc.)*

A Bairn's Sang

Roun' an' aroun' an three times three;
Polly an' Peg an' Pansy:
Roun' an' aroun the muckle tree;
An' its roun' a' the wurld whan ye gang wi' me
Roun' the merry-metanzie.
An' its roun' a' the wurld whan ye gang wi' me
Roun' the merry-metanzie.

The wind blaws heich an' the wind blaws lang;
Polly an' Peg an' Pansy:
Blaw, wind, blaw as we lilt oor sang;
For it's roun' a' the wurld whan wi me ye gang
Roun the merry-metanzie.
For it's roun' a' the wurld whan wi me ye gang
Roun' the merry-metanzie.

The Tattie-Bogle

(2 tattiebogles, 4 speaking)

The tattie-bogle wags his airms:
Caw! Caw! Caw!
He hasna onie banes or thairms:
Caw! Caw! Caw!

We corbies wha hae taken tent,
And wamphl'd round, and glower'd asklent,
Noo gang hame lauchin owre the bent:
Caw! Caw! Caw!

The Auld Man o Muckhart
(two acting)

The auld man o' Muckhart
sae boo-backit is he
That whan he dovers owre
His neb is on his knee:

And whan he stechers oot
He gowks atween his legs:
"Hoch!" girns the auld man:
"It's grand for getherin eggs."

"What'll ye dae, what'll ye dae,
Gin ye grow waur and waur?"
"Hoch!" yapps the auld man:
"I'll hae to gang on fower."
"What'll ye dae, what'll ye dae,
Whan ye canna stap ava?"
"Hoch!" lauchs the auld man:
"I'll birl like a ba'."

Aince Upon a Day
(duet)

Aince upon a day my mither said to me:
Dinna cleip and dinna rype
And dinna tell a lee.
For gin ye cleip a craw will name ye,
And gin ye rype a daw will shame ye;

And a snail will heeze its hornies out
And hike them round and round aboot
gin ye tell a lee.

Aince upon a day, as I walkit a' my lane,
I met a daw and monie a craw,
And a snail upon a stane.
Up gaed the daw and didna shame me:
Up gaed ilk craw and didna name me:
But the wee snail heez'd its hornies out
And hik'd them round and round about
and – goggl'd at me.

The Drucken Fuggie-Toddler
(act out)

The fuggie-toddler's bummin-fou:
Bumbleleerie bum:
The fuggie-toddler's bummin-fou
Wi' swackin up the hinny-dew:
Bumbleleerie bum,
Bum, bum.

He styters here and styters there:
Bumbleleerie bum:
He styters here and styters there,
And canna styter onie mair:
Bumbleleerie bum,
Bum, bum.

And doun ablow a daisy-fleur:
Bumbleleerie bum:
And doun ablow a daisy-fleur
He havers owre and owre and owre:
Bumbleleerie bum,
Bum, bum.

Dreepin Weather
(all)

Out stapp't the ae duck;
Out stapp't anither;
Out stappit a' the ducks
To take the dreepin weather.

Diddle-doddl'd through the dubs
Flappin wi' their feet:
O! the bonnie gutter-holes
And the weet, weet, weet!

During the next poem, as if under a spell, all the children gravitate to Soutar's bed, and by the end of the poem are asleep on Soutar's bed. Soutar B is standing behind, watching.

Day Is Dune

Soutar A: Lully, lully, my ain wee dearie:
Lully, lully, my ain wee doo;
Sae far awa and peerieweerie
Is the hurlie o' the world noo.

And a' the noddin pows are weary;
And a' the fitterin feet come in:
Lully, lully, my ain wee dearie,
The darg is owre and the day is düne.

Lights fade. Exit children. The lighting here should be very subdued. Evelyn goes and stand beside Soutar B, and says to him directly:

Eve: Hairst the licht o' the müne
To mak a siller goun;
And the gowdan licht o' the sün
To mak a pair o shoon:

Soutar B takes Evelyn's hand, and leads her down to the front of stage, crouches down, and recites the rest of the poem.

Soutar B: Gether the draps o' dew
To hing about your throat;
And the wab o' the watergaw
To wark yoursel' a coat:

And you will ride oniewhaur
Upon the back o' the wind;
And gang through the open door
In the wa' at the world's end.

Act ll Scene 3

Lights up. Soutar A in bed, Soutar B observing.

Soutar A: Often, often, I'm afraid, I play the spider to my friends:
Soutar B: "Will you walk into my bedroom,"
        said the spider to the flies;
    "Will you open out your spirits
        that I may anatomize
    "With my little inky scalpel
        till each fad, or foible, lies
    "Naked to the daylight
        or your own awaken'd eyes;
    "Now I ask you,"
Soutar A: says the spider,
Soutar B: "what are your replies?'
Soutar A: "Pick your own bones, Mr. Spider,
    won't you get a damn surprise,
    "And when you've had your pickings
    you can leave them for the flies."

Over the twelve days of Christmas, 1931, I had visits from about 40 people, some of whom came twice! *(sounding exhausted)* It seemed all the birds were migrating this way. Mums gave me a pair of owl-bookends, one friend a kookaburra matchbox holder, someone else a cockatoo ashtray – and –

Soutar B: – Mrs MacKenzie's enormous chocolate parrot!

Soutar A: Do they think I am a love-sick dodo? Yes, it was a Merry Christmas.

Enter minister, with handle-bar moustache and a pompous, though Scots, manner

Minister: *(unaware that he's being tactless)* Hello there, Willie. Hou are ye daein. It's a grand day for walkin.

Soutar A: Ay, I'm sure it is! Hou's yersel!

Minister: Grand, grand, never better. It's a pity that nooadays ye canna come tae the Kirk.

Soutar A: *(lying)* It is that!

Minister: But nae maitter: the Kirk can come to you! And so, here I am, tae cheer ye up.

Soutar A: That's gey guid o ye, John.

Minister: I'm shair ye're richt. I brocht alang ma new pipe tae show ye. I ken ye like the baccy yersel. It's a beauty!

He brings out an enormous pipe and hands it to Soutar, takes it back, and proceeds to puff away.

Soutar A: Help ma Boab! That's a fell muckle contraption.

Minister: Ye dinna mind if I juist hae a wee bit smoke?

Soutar A: No, of course not...

The minister puffs away, talking non stop to Soutar, who becomes overwhelmed by the smoke. After a few seconds [about an hour in 'real' time], he gets up. By this time Soutar is visibly choking.

Soutar B: He'll turn my room into the very womb of obfuscation! I'll hae tae develop a cough. *(he makes a magician-like gesture. Soutar A immediately coughs)*

Minister: Weill, I'll hae tae be awa. I've still tae visit Mrs Macrae who's got the bronchitis! Why, man, Soutar, ye're coughing. Ye dinna hae a touch o the bronchitis yersel! *(Soutar B shakes his head, animatedly)* That's fine. Guid day tae ye. Glad to see ye're sae weill. See you next week. *(he goes out)*

Soutar B: I'd raither see him in yon place first.

Enter a young, attractive woman with small, nervous gestures.

Moira: *(brightly)* Hello Willie, how are ye today?

Soutar A: I'm fine, and yersel?

Moira: Grand. I've just got word o a new job, starting as an assistant in McEwans on Monday, working in the haberdashery section.

Soutar A: Great stuff! That'll be yer immediate problems solved.

Moira: Ay, that's right. My mither said tae tell ye that old Mrs Broun is fair no weill. She said ye uised tae visit her.

Soutar A: I did that, when I wis a bairn. Wud ye ask yer mither tae say tae Mrs Broun that I wis asking for her...

Moira mutters on.

Soutar B: Nou if a poet could work on a body as on a poem, I could mak Moira intae a beauty. She has the features, hair and complexion – but the eyes are smaa and her movements nervous.

Ah! the dignity, the repose, of Greek sculpture. I wonder, if Moira looked eneuch there, wad she find classic grace... *(becoming self-critical)* Whit a bigheid I am...

Enter an elderly lady: Miss Black, a friendly but righteous soul.

Soutar A: Hello, Miss Black. Please to see you!

Miss Black: Ye're lookin weill. Is aathin fine?

Soutar A: I'm fine. The most robust invalid in Perth, that's me.

Miss Black: Eh, Willie, it's you that's aye cheery. Coming to see you aye maks me feel better – though I dinna ken how it leaves you.

Soutar A: *(reassuringly)* Oh, much cheerier, much cheerier, Miss Black.

Miss Black: That new minister's guid. I cam awa quite upliftit. I aye felt with the last minister that his knowledge of theology and the Bible wisnae just quite whit it should be.

Soutar B: Wi her bein an Auld maid and an Auld Licht, we couldnae get past the kirk. I sit in a semicircle o withered virgins. Aa nice women, but I'd give onything tae see a proper beauty...

Soutar A: Of course, there's no mony ken as muckle as you, Miss Black.

Miss Black: Oh nonsense, I'm juist an auld wifie. I dinna ken as muckle as ony minister.

Soutar A: I'm sure that's no true, Miss Black...

Miss Black: *(laughing nervously, but with pleasure)* Oh, I'll be on my way rejoicing! *(exits)*

Enter a mean-looking type. He sits down and begins to hold forth.

Soutar B: This man is beginnin tae get on my nerves. As a type, he's interesting – but his meanness, like a skeleton, seems tae thrust itself through his skin. He likes sneering better than praising. There is a rigidness about aa his gestures, as if the mean spirit denied ony generosity o movement tae his body.

Mr Brown: I'll be going now, Willie. I'm glad ye agree wi me about the sad state o the Kirk session. They winna listen tae me. Mr Smith, wha taks the minutes o the meetings, canna even spell.

Soutar A: That'll no dae then, eh Mr Broun?

Mr Brown: Cheerio Willie. I'll be alang next week, tae gie ye a wee bit cheer. *(he goes out)*

Soutar B: My God, my God, it's a death sentence!

Soutar A: I sit here sinkin deeper intae silence like a houlat that's lost its moose while the talk flows on like a back-lade. I'll tell him that one visit a month maun be the maximum.

Soutar B: O Boy! I'll seem a thankless brute. *(re-enter Mr Brown)*

Mr Brown: Hello Willie, terrible day, isn't it?

Soutar A: Quite terrible, Mr Broun.

Soutar B: I feel a chronic congestion in my chest, and want to cry out, 'Go! Go! Go!'

Mr Brown: Have ye seen the P.A. this week, Willie? *(Soutar A shakes his head, dumb with misery)* Well, the council are proposin tae spend hunners o pounds makin a park up at Jeanfield for the bairns tae play in. Whit's wrang wi them pleyin in the streets?

Soutar B: *(aside)* Can't he read my face! Can't he see what I'm really saying – Christ! When will this man leave me!

Mr Brown: And they're diggin up the road again, doun at the South Street. I widnae mind, but it's the ratepayers that have tae foot the bill... I'll be alang next Tuesday... *(exit during next speech)*

Soutar B: *(aside)* And I'm shair to be here awaitin him. He thinks: "Poor chap, so cut off from the outside world, I'll hop over and cheer him up – he'll be delighted to see me! – Will I hell! I wish it could be like this:

Enter a woman dressed only in underwear. She and Soutar B embrace, kiss and laugh, rather lustily. Enter Mr Brown.

Mr Brown: *(not noticing the woman, but proceeding immediately with his small talk)* It's me again, Wullie. I juist had tae come an tell you – we've discovered that the minister has sired an illegitimate bairn..

Soutar A: *(clearing his throat)* A-hem. *(bringing forward the girl)* Oh, hello, Mr Brown – I haven't introduced you to my friend. *(she is lying across his bed)* This is Dolly, my mistress. *(she waves coquettishly at him)*

Mr Brown: *(eyeing her up and down with a mixture of disgust, horror and lust)* Well, really! Willie Soutar! If you're goin tae go hoorin yer wey tae hell an damnation... ye'll get nae mair visits fae me!

Soutar A: *(triumphantly)* Success! *(the fantasy leaves Soutar chuckling with good humour)* How can I complain: most of my visitors are the salt of the earth, but! 20 hours a week of meaningless conversation. And I can't even talk to them aboot poetry. Now, if I could walk abroad and speak with scavengers, bargees, tramps and any chance traveller – talk might become an adventure. But a couple of hours to mysel is like gold-dust: how subtle is self-flattery. What am I tacitly sayin tae sae mony o my friends: "When you leave me I shall be in much better company."

Reader: Soutar the poet used to lie
           And brood upon divinity;
           Until, in meditative birth,
           This aphorism was bodied forth: -
           "God and humanity are one."
           He took his pen to write it down;
           But, having heard the front-door bell,
           Shut fast his book and mutter'd

Soutar A: "Hell!"
(after a pause) The routine was endless and wearying, an infinity of trivial tasks for my parents. And for me... agonies. You cannae divorce the body and mind – a poem disnae come easy when ye're in pain. Yesterday when I looked oot on the daffodils, I micht as weill hae been looking on a row o bricks. *(pause)*

Soutar is writing his diary. He reads it out. The mood to try to create is one of intense concentration on the diarist's words.

Soutar B: This diary of mine became an obsession. I wonder if any of it'll ever see the light of day. Who'd be interested in the daily mind-flow of a pokerstiff invalid?

Soutar A: *(reading the entry)* September, Monday 15th: Yesterday morning Eve found a hedgehog on our step at the side-door. Brought it up on a shovel to let me see it. Wasn't very frightened. Dark beady eyes. We left a saucer of milk for it.

Soutar B: Tuesday 16th: Milk all gone from the saucer we left for hedgehog – but how are we to know it was the hedgehog who enjoyed it? *(he shrugs his shoulders at the audience)*

Soutar A: October, Wednesday 1st: Began reading through the Encyclopaedia Britannica today. Another ten years project, at least.

Soutar B: Finished reading a brochure by Lawrence, entitled 'Apropos Lady Chatterley's Lover'. I haven't got the book, of course. Damn the police – 'hired' critics.

The rest can be taken by various readers.

After playing an instrument my own 'chords' seem 'tuned up' ready for melody. Last night after playing the whistle I surprised myself at how well I was whistling. I'm a good whistler – but last night I'd a range, a smoothness and control, I don't normally have. I enjoyed myself.

Professor Grierson seems to have kept in mind how poetry had 'interfered' with my studies. Might have said whether he thinks that I'm justifying my choice – in spite of him!

Eve in for yarns "from my dead self".

The whistling of birds is more rumbustious now they sense the awakening of spring and we also must respond to day and day. A man is so moulded by the diurnal aspect of earth and sky. The dust of a shire is in our bones and its seasonable beauty in our spirit – so when a man says that he *belongs* to this or that place he is often speaking more truly than he knows.

Our new maid thinks I'm good looking. Whoopee – a fat lot of comfort that is: song for melodramatic baritone: Will was a handsome fellow and all the girls loved Will: But he lay too long in a single bed – and that's why he's single still. *(both Soutars chuckle)*

A diary is the introvert's exhibitionism, leaving his little self exposed to a stranger's gaze in the hope that the living might bide a moment with the dead and not condemn. Poor, expectant diarist – what's your ghost listening for – is it to hear a still warm voice saying: "I wish I had known this man."

Sometimes when I turn out the pocket of my mind I find my thoughts are like sticky caramels. (both Soutars grimace).

As I enter up my thought for each day on the day following there can be no entry for the day on which I die. Let me write it down now. "To accept life is to give it beauty."

How easy to become peevish in prison. Ella McQueen, if she is in the garden, usually gives me a wave – today she didn't and I felt annoyed. Silly ass.

Russell McQueen – the little boy next door, referring to *Junior*

Reader in Scots: "I see Rabbie Burns is coming on now – he's included in the same anthology as you."

Soutar B: Why do I feel it worth while to fill up a page such as this day by day?

Soutar A: Because I can't go out and chop a basket of firewood or take the weeds out of the garden path?'

Soutar B: Yet that wouldn't be a wholly honest answer. We are all sustained at times by the thought that, whatever we may be, not a single other creature in all the history of the world has been just as ourself – not another will be like us. Why not put on record something of the world as seen by this lonely 'ego': here and there, perhaps, a sentence may be born whose father is reality.

Soutar A: Of course, a lot of trivia: Odds forenoon. Dinner. Odds. Listened in to the beginning of the Rugger International – but soon lost interest. Odd writing. Tea early. Folks off to the Stirlings to spend the evening. Odds. Wrote a little thing in Scots called *'The Tryst':*

Blackout. Soutar B comes down to the edge of the stage: 'The Tryst'

Soutar B: O luely, luely cam she in
    And luely she lay doun:
    I kent her be her caller lips
    And her breists sae sma' and roun'.

    A' thru the nicht we spak nae word
    Nor sinder'd bane frae bane:
    A' thru the nicht I heard her hert
    Gang soundin' wi my ain.

    It was about the waukrife hour
    Whan cocks begin to craw
    That she smool'd saftly thru the mirk
    Afore the day wud daw.

    Sae luely, luely cam she in
    Sae luely was she gaen
    And wi' her a' my simmer days
    Like they had never been.

Soutar and Eve playing at riddles:

Soutar A: Riddle me ree – now let me see

Soutar B: I am ae thing:
I am nae thing:
Baith a big and sma' thing;
And belang to a' thing.

Eve: I know what it is: it's a shadow!

Soutar A: Right first time. Try this one:

Soutar B: Yon laddie wi' the gowdan pow
Sae braw in the simmer sün
Will wag a head as white as tow
Afore the year is düne.

The leaf will fa', and the blustery blaw
That birls the leaf in the air
Will rive his linty locks awa
And lave him bell and bare.

Eve: An old man!

Soutar A: No – try again! Here's a clue. It's a weed!

Eve: I know – a dandelion! Hurray! Now can we have the Bible-games.

Soutar A: The one where we change the names of all the characters in the Bible.

Eve: That's it! Can I start? Moses?

Soutar A: Toeses! – just like the tootsies you've got!

Eve: Here's a really hard one: Nebucadnezar.

Soutar A: Next-in-the-shed,-sir! *(peals of laughter)* Here's a hard one for you – Ham, Shem and Japheth.

Eve: Ham *(she looks doubtfully at Soutar)*

Soutar A: Carry on then, see whit ye dae wi the rest o it!

Eve: Ham, Jam and Half-loaf!

Soutar A: Very guid. Gie me anither yin:

Eve: Shadrak, Mishak and Abednigo!

Soutar A: Ye wee mischief! Let me see! ...I've got it! Hayrick!.. Sea-sick! and – To-bed-you-go!! *(Eve cheers and they both laugh)* Oh Eve?

Eve: Yes?

Soutar A: You're playing the fairy-godmother in the play at the Girls Guildry tomorrow night, aren't you?

Eve: Yes.

Soutar A: Weill look, I made this for you. *(he produces a glittery star on the end of a stick)*

Eve: That's great! Thank you, Willie! *(she kisses him)*

Soutar A: OK. Off you go...

Eve: Is it really my bed-time!

Soutar A: Nearly!

Eve: Willie, me and my pals would like to make you the President of our club!

Soutar A: Hoo-roo! Whit a privilege! What's your club called?

Eve: The ROSEBUDS.

Soutar A: My conscience! Me! President of the Rosebuds. Well, I'm rosy enough, God wot.

Eve: Will you, Willie *(laughing at her own pun)*

Soutar A: Of course I will. Thank you for conferring so high an honour on me. Oh! I've something else for you. Hand me that book over there.

Eve: It's called 'Seeds in the Wind'.

Soutar A: Open it up. Look at the page at the front. See who it's dedicated to?

Eve: Eh?

Soutar A: Guess!

Eve: The King!

Soutar A: No – someone much more important.

Eve: Who?

Soutar A: To Eve.

Eve: *(non-plussed)* Oh!

Eve runs up stage in a mixture of delight, embarrassment and confusion.

Act II Scene 4

Readers: Caledonia's near a corp;
Puir auld Caledonie:
Scrog and skrank wi' English slorp
And English parsimony.

What can mak our Scotland hale:
What mak her braw and bonnie?
Hamely brose and hamely kail,
Bannock and baup and sconie?

Wauk her wi' a Doric sang;
Dirl her wi' the dronie:
She'll come tae hersel' or lang
And gang as gleg as onie.

Gin she were hersel' aince mair
(And this is no a ronie)
A' the world wud wark to share
The rowth o' Caledonie.

Soutar A: I'm lucky. I'm driven by a force ayont mysell. It thrusts a compulsive finger intae the middle o my spine and drives me on. Now the spirit o Scotland and the warld is in travail – and the struggle has passed into my ain flesh and blood. I've found at last the symbol I need: the unicorn. I've somethin in common wi that beast: its solitariness and self-will, for whit else has sustained me? But I also identify the unicorn wi Scotland, wi oor re-awakened nationalism: it gaithers strength and potency as it ramps through the imagination. If I control it, may it no dance for a nation?

Unicorn descends behind

Reader:　　Look up; and yonder on the brae,
Like a sang in silence born,
Wi' the dayspring o' the day
Walks the snaw-white unicorn.

Sae far awa he leams in licht;
And yet his glitter burns atween
The darkness hung ahint the hicht
And hidden in the lifted e'en.

Look doun and doun; frae ilka airt
The flutherin worlds through darkness fa';
But yon bricht beast walks, in the hert,
Sae far awa, sae far awa.

Soutar B: English isnae natural tae me; I use it 'consciously' even in conversation; aften I feel I'm speakin a foreign language. My mature poetry was born when I turned tae Scots. But I worry that my efforts, and MacDiarmid's, micht be owre late:

Reader: Nae man wha loves the lawland tongue
But warsles wi' the thocht –
There are mair sangs that bide unsung
Nor a' that hae been wrocht.

Ablow the wastrey o' the years,
The thorter o' himsel',
Deep buried in his bluid he hears
A music that is leal.

And wi' this lealness gangs his ain;
And there's nae ither gait
Though a' his feres were fremmit men
Wha cry: *Owre late, owre late.*

Soutar B: MacDiarmid and I hae been caa'd 'dictionary delvers' – as if we just dug up deid words and stuck them doun onyhow in the kailyaird. The dictionary is a country our fathers possessed and we return there to find what we've lost but retain as a memory in the blood. We're like an artist wanderin amang the crowd looking for this face or that to become a pairt o a great canvas. We know whit we want to find – our discovery is no by chance, but a corroboration o oor ain intuition.

Reader: The Solitary Place

As through the wilderness he gaed,
The stanes spak oot to speer his need:
"The mercy o the world," he said.

Rocks in their pity cried: "What pack
O' naethingness boos doun your back?"
"The mercy o' the world, alack."

Atween his tatters blench'd the bane:
Frae ilka airt wail'd the cauld win':
"The mercy o' the warld blaws in."

And through the hollow o' his hand
He watch'd the sinderin drift o' sand:
A lane man in a lanely land.

Soutar B: As guid as the best o MacDiarmid's lyrics ... *(chuckles)*

Enter MacDiarmid, dressed in full Highland dress and slightly inebriated.

MacDiarmid: Whit's this nonsense, Soutar? I've said that next tae mysel ye're the best poet in Scotland, but I dispute ony suggestion that yon poem can haud a caunnle tae the best o ma work.

Soutar A: I'm no arguin wi ye aboot it. This is no a duel wi couplets at ten paces!

MacDiarmid: If it were, Soutar, ye'd find the pea-shooter o yer verse had some difficulty matchin my blast o cannon-fire.

Soutar A: I ken ye dinna like Biblical parallels, but I micht remind ye o the story o David and Goliath. David's peashooter o a sling wis mair nor a match for aa Goliath's strength. Ye've lost aa sense o comeliness in a poem. Ye've got great energy, I ken – I wish I had as muckle – but ye should mind that tae become a star, ye hae tae pass ayont nebulosity.

MacDiarmid: Ye mak a guid flyting, Soutar. But I reckon that as a poet, bairnrhymes are aboot your level. Ye could never dae onythin as elevated in conception as my 'Water Music'.

Soutar A: I can't understand how a man who suggested, as you did, that I cluttered up the sense o ma poems in Scots by using owre mony Scots words could write sic a spate of incomprehensibility as 'Water Music'. It's a pity that you – Scotland's leading poet – suld sacrifice quality for quantity.

MacDiarmid: At least ye ken yer place, Soutar. Ye juist dinna hae the same kind o' poetic ambitions. Ye're owre thirled tae the ballad, which hasnae the scope for the kind of poetry I want. And the ballads ye write are mair like hymns than ballads. And as for yer 'Vocable Verses': they're nocht but trivia set to metre.

Soutar A: My vocable verses are the lumber room that micht hae smoored my poetry in rubbish. Your poetry wad be better o a similar dustbin.

MacDiarmid: Truce, Soutar – yer independent spirit and guid nature juist confirm my opinion o yersel as the ainly ither poet in Scotland I hae ony time for. Noo, I'd like to read you a bit o my new pamphlet 'Red Scotland'. *(He pulls a quarter bottle out of his sporran and takes a slug.)*

MacDiarmid is bending lower and lower over Soutar's bed, dropping cigarette ash all over it

Soutar A: Stop! Stop! Tak yer fag ash and dialectical materialism awa fae me. It's enough tae put me aff socialism for life!

MacDiarmid: Will ye no collaborate wi me on this anthology after the communist ideal "a comprehensive celebration of Scottish working-class life, past and present"? Ye're the yin man in Scotland that is up to sic a challenge.

Soutar A: Naw, Christopher. I'm flattered ye think sae, despite oor flyting, but I'm also no sae shair that ma poetry *is* up tae it. I've aye fand it difficult tae write tae order.

MacDiarmid: You're too modest, Soutar.

Soutar A: Not at aa. Yer idea's guid, but there's yin problem wi't You want to write the working class's poems for them – and I dinna believe ye can dae that. Ye're assuming the working class canna tak the responsibility themsels – and that's the auld capitalist presumption that the common man is no tae be trusted wi *full* self-responsibility.

MacDiarmid: There's truith in whit ye say, but ye forget that I am from the working, peasant classes, as much as ye are, tho yer faimly has elevated itsel recently.

Soutar A: Ye may be *from* the workin class, but ye hae tae mind that ye're *no* the *haill* o the workin class.

MacDiarmid: And why no? I've created modern Scottish literature, single-handed.

Soutar A: *(laughing)* – not quite.

MacDiarmid catches a glimpse of himself in one of Soutar's mirrors. Throughout the next lines of dialogue, he keeps looking admiringly at himself in the mirror.

Soutar A: Onywey, are ye quite collected again eftir yer spell at Gilgal. I was worried aboot you last time I saw you.

MacDiarmid: Mental asylums are no place for poets – though Gilgal is better than maist. The doctors think I could go back to Shetland soon.

Soutar A: Weill, at least you get peace there tae write, which is mair than I dae here.

MacDiarmid: Ye ken, Willie, *(looking at himself in the mirror and preening himself)*. I think this deathly pallor rather becomes me!

MacDiarmid comes forward and speaks to the audience.

MacDiarmid: Soutar's amazing serenity of spirit, the fineness of his character, and his freedom from all trace of rancour or repining was what struck me most on each occasion we met. No doubt that was the impression of himself he gave continuously, but the truth of the matter was far from so simple. The serene acceptance was only the polish – the surface of the steel. Under the bland acceptance he always maintained, there was a very tough and tortured character indeed. *(He exits.)*

Soutar B: He's right. I am a moody man, although few ken it, and a moody man is one who overestimates his ain importance. Sometimes I have to remind myself, 'Look here, wee man – even if the universe turns around you, it turned round juist the same afore you were born – and will turn lang eftir you are deid! And I maun pay tribute to Grieve: a bonnier fechter Scotland never saw and if there is a new Scotland, a braver spirit abroad these days, it's mair due tae him that tae onybody else – includin masel.

Soutar A: Being sae dependent on loving help, I understaun the suffering o folk wha depend on unwillin or vindictive aid. My body is nae langer my ain private possession: it maun be haunelt and directed by ithers. My dreams are still haunted by women. I realise that if my folks were dead, I wad marry if I could – and I believe that a woman wad accept me for whit I am. But as my journey becomes mair lanesome, distressed and burdensome, my desire for sexual completion is mair compelling that ever. But are we not maist fond, maist eident, when we maun say fareweel?

Enter John Soutar.

John Soutar: Willie, I've juist been up Callerfountain. I've brocht ye this. It's watter frae the burn up there.

Soutar A: You minded my three wishes, Pops.

They look at each other with a little embarrassment at the emotion they both feel. Soutar breaks the silence with a teasing chuckle

Go on then, are ye gaunnae gie me a draft o't.

John pours him out a glassful and hands it to him.

John Soutar: There ye are.

Soutar A: Mmm, *(he gives a sigh of satisfaction)* No sae icy as I expected it to be ... but guid! Thank ye.

Enter James Finlayson

Soutar B: Finnel wis yin o ma maist regular and welcome visitors.

Soutar A: I hear the Scottish National Party's daein weel these days.

Finlayson: I still haven't enlisted. An I winna enlist!

Soutar A: I've stuck to the ideal of an independent Scotland for years, but I'm no signing up with ony political party. MacDiarmid tries to enroll me with the Communists and though I'm convinced o the rightness o socialism, I winna go that road either.

Finlayson: The thirties have been a bleak time: unemployment, the growing shadow of events in Europe – the Spanish Civil War. Scotland needs its ain voice these days. It's more important than ever that we declare independence.

Soutar A: I begin to feel oppressed by the political events o the last few years: the poverty, urban squalor. *(He hands Jim a sheet.)*

Soutar B: Doun by the Clyde there is a skeleton
       That ne'er had a body: a ghost gaen deid
       Afore it cam alive. It micht hae won
       Its way, owre the wurld's waters, or the weed
       O' time tax't abune it; nane then carin'
       Sin it had come thru the storm o' the years:
       But yon thing, neither a corp nor a bairn,
       Rots in the womb. Wha looks upon it peers
       On mair than he sees – gin he but look richt:
       Ayont they iron banes gang the Glasgow wyndes
       Fou o' sic skeletons, waesome tae the sicht
       That sklents unner the skulls and meets the minds.
       Day eftir day they walk owre Glasgow Green
       An' the wurds they speak are no what the mouth
       Speaks but the e'en – an' ahint the e'en –
       Cryin', cryin': What hae ye dune tae oor youth.

Finlayson: That's powerful stuff – but no your usual at all.

Soutar A: Maybe my Muse is too rural – but coming from Perth, with hills and greenery aa roun, the industrial horrors o the Clyde are sae far awa they seem in anither universe.

Finlayson: The trouble is that the principles of the Scottish National Party are too diffuse – too weak!

Soutar A: *(slightly wryly)* Oh, Jim, whit wey 'too weak', ye're no lookin fur racial purity, are ye?

Finlayson: Well, I despise what Hitler is doing in Germany, but if we can bring out the racial differences of the Scots from the English and others, we would release a spirit which would be stronger and more confident than we find in Scotland the day.

Soutar A: *(speaking in jest, but happening to hit the nail on the head)* But that's what MacDiarmid and I are doing, through poetry, trying to gie the Scots language back to the people. You canna dae it by telling folk they're really Picts!

Finlayson: Well, I think the ancient Picts had the answer. Look at the ingeniousness of the old brochs. If we're to be Scots, we have to get back to these Pictish roots.

Soutar A: I think we'll find the answer in the poetry o Dunbar and Henrysoun, even in Burns – and especially in MacDiarmid. We'll find it by encouraging people in our ain time to get tae ken the Scots traditions and tak them intae the 20th century.

Finlayson: No, Soutar, you're wrang. That's just like pouring a pint of beer which is nothing but the froth on the top. I've got the answer. *(He scrabbles in his briefcase.)* Here it is *(He waves a paper aloft.)* The Official Programme of the Pict Party.

Soutar A: And how mony members o this bonnie party dae ye hae?

Finalyson: Five – but that's no matter. Once people get to hear about this, they'll come flocking.

Soutar A: Absolute rot! It's an irresponsible digression, diverting folk from what really matters now: social deprivation – yes – Scottish nationalism but as a pairt o a larger vision – and then, there's war, the largest o the mental slums we hae tae win free frae the noo. Agin that, yer concern wi the Picts looks like a silly obsession wi tiddlywinks!

Finlayson: *(angry and hurt)* I never thought that you of all people would be so unsympathetic to anything Scottish!

Soutar A: I'm no unsympathetic, I just think ye're wrang, dangerously wrang in your priorities. The blackest storm ye could imagine is gaitherin abuin our heids, and you sit, ostrichlike, wi yer heid stuck in a Pictish broch. And it's war like we've never seen afore. The Spanish Civil War has filled me wi horror: Guernica – the cold-bluided extermination o a haill community, women – and worse – bairns.

Soutar B or Reader/s:

> Upon the street they lie
> Beside the broken stone
> The blood of the children stares from the broken stone.
>
> Death came out of the sky
> In the bright afternoon:
> Darkness slanted over the bright afternoon.
>
> Again the sky is clear
> but upon earth a stain:
> The earth is darkened with a darkening stain:
>
> A wound which is everywhere
> Corrupts the hearts of men:
> The blood of children corrupts the hearts of men.
>
> Silence is in the air:
> The stars move to their places:
> Silent and serene the stars move to their places:
>
> But from earth the children stare
> With blind and fearful faces:
> And our charity is in the children's faces.

Finlayson: *(slightly mollified)* That's a fine poem, Willie, but watch, ye'll be arguing yoursel intae pacifism next.

Soutar A: I already have.

Finlayson: Soutar, ye've gane gyte! A man who's a pacifist in time of war is a traitor, or a coward.

Soutar A: No. At the ruit o pacifism is a trust in mankind. So as pacifism is an act o faith – you either pit your trust in force – or in the ultimate brotherhood o men – and if it's tae be that, then no tae fight is a creative – indeed a moral act!

Finlayson: We'll just have to disagree about all that. In my mind all pacifists are feardygowks – there can be no other explanation. Anyway, yer pacifist freend Chamberlain's got Hitler all sewn up. And ony man that denies the true origins of Scotland can be nae friend of mine. *(He exits)*

Soutar B: *(angry)*

> There were four cooks, ho! very fine cooks,
> Who met to make a plot:
> Adolph and Musso and Ladeeda
> And the flying Chamberpot.

Wind and lies, wind and lies,
And a mesmerising smell,
They muddled and mixed; muddled and mixed;
Muddled and mixed them well...

Now, from the Czech, our Jason lifts a fleece
To be the German dragon's robe of peace;
And, in his folly, dreams the traitorous deed
Has reft the monster of his hungry seed!

Act II Scene 4

Soutar A: I mind the strangest visitation I ever had, on the 4th of September, 1939, the night after war was declared. That night, a woman friend o mine, made mad by the horror o it aa, cam tappin at the window – before even the dawn light was in the sky. She refused to go away wi'oot seein me.

Enter an anonymous female figure, mid-thirties. She carries in her left hand a little bunch of flowers, containing a single sycamore leaf, a spray of yellow calceolarias, and a yellow rose.

Woman: God has sent me with a message for Willie.

She walks over to the bed and takes Soutar B's hand in hers. She looks up in an attitude of prayer and says with great earnestness

Woman: Father, give me the words. *(she pauses, as if trying to make contact with the Almighty, then says haltingly)* Go to Middleton Murray ... and tell him to go to Iona ... . You can rise up ... . Say 'God makes me well'.

Soutar A: *(seriously)* God makes me well.

Woman: God make me well and save my soul from hell ... *(She passes her hand over Soutar's brow)* Jesus is married now ... I am Christ in female form.

Like a minister uplifting a chalice at the altar, she lifts up her bouquet.

Woman: Here is the rose, the symbol of immortality.

She detaches the rose from the bouquet and gives it to Soutar, who gravely accepts it

Here is the sycamore, the symbol of immortality.

She detaches the sycamore leaf from the bouquet and hands it to Soutar.

Soutar A: *(almost whispering)* Thank you.

Woman: And these little yellow calceolarias will bring back life to your limbs ... You can rise up now. I shan't watch you.

She turns slowly away and moves downstage, saying softly to herself:

Jesus is married now ... I am Christ in female form ... Yellow leaf, yellow flowers, gold like the sun ... God makes you well ... You can rise up now ... remember ...

Soutar B: *(aside)* And, miraculously, I felt my muscles ease. I had to try to bend my back and move my legs to convince myself that a miracle hadn't happened ...

Woman: Will you give me money to go to Iona – I must go there.

Soutar A: Of course. If you come back later today, I'll have it for you.

Woman: Thank you. *(she looks round)* I'll go now.

Soutar A: Take care of yourself.

Woman: *(puzzled – slowly)* But – I haven't any self ... *(exits)*

Soutar B: *(moving thoughtfully back to the audience)* Wi the dawn light, it was as if it had been a dream, but the fragrance o the rose filled the room ... Whit a wonderful gift she tried tae gie me, my puir deranged Ophelia ... I wadna play the Hamlet wi you, banish ye tae a nunnery. I'd have gaithered you in my arms and cared for you. I wantit tae heal yer scattered wits, disturbed by a world on the brink o war ...

Throughout this last sequence, we should feel more strongly than ever the palpable bond between the two Soutars, as they gradually grow closer together.

Soutar A: I've had a long time to accustom myself to silence and solitude, but even now desire troubles me. Yet it means there's creativity still alive in me. The earth's loveliness has become quintessential in woman. For me three images remain as doors into fuller life: woman, tree and unicorn, which I honour wi a crown o silence:

Soutar B: The hert may be sae rowth wi' sang
It has nae need to sing;
The e'en sae lichtit as owregang
The sicht o' oniething:

A' the roch rummage o' the world
Dwin'd to a dinnlin bell:
A the dark warsle o' the world
Ingether'd and stane-still.

Soutar A: I ken nou the sweetness of life, its sanctity. The chill shade o death ower the world touches me tae the quick. In desperate opposition the flesh craves contact wi anither human being, to assert the triumph o life in the midst o death and destruction.

Soutar B: No man outlives the grief of war
Though he outlive its wreck
Upon the memory a scar
Through all his years will ache.

Hopes will revive when horrors cease;
And dreaming dread be stilled;
But there shall dwell within his peace
A sadness unannulled.

Upon his world shall hang a sign
Which summer cannot hide:
The permanence of the young men
Who are not by his side.

Soutar A: My pacifism and international outlook has lost me yin o ma dearest friends. Jim wrote the other day to accuse me of washing my hands, like Pilate, over the truth that confronted me in the Pict Party Programme. I'll write a conciliatory letter, athout retracting what I said – I doot if he'll reply ...

Reader: November Wednesday 4th: 1942

Sic a hoast hae I got
Sic a hoast hae I got
I dout my days are on the trot;
Sic a hoast hae I got.

Whauzlin like an auld tup,
I grup whatever's there to grup

> And clocher half my stummick up;
> Sic a hoast hae I got.
>
> The delver at his deathly trade
> Gies a rattle wi' his spade;
> Blinks an e'e, and shaks his head;
> Sic a hoast hae I got.

Soutar A: Pneumonia, of course.

Soutar B: Tuesday 15th December:

Soutar A: Began smoking again after a lapse o mair than five weeks – hadn't much pleasure from the few cigarettes I savoured: staleness has permeated most things.

Soutar B: May, Wednesday 12, 1943:
Historic date – definitely stopped smoking.

Soutar A: For many years Tobac and I
Have been to each a faithful friend
And now, without a single sigh,
Our comradeship is at an end.

Soutar B: July, Sunday 4th:

Soutar A: D. B. Low looked in at 11.30. After a sounding, he said there was a cavity at the apex of my right lung – I take this as a death sentence.

Reader: They delv'd a saft hole
For Johnnie McNeel:
He aye had been droll
But folk likit him weel.

On a wee, mossy-knoll,
That's green a' the year,
A stane-letter'd scroll
Tells Johnnie liggs there.

Nae lang rigmarole;
Juist – Johnnie McNeel
Was aye a bit droll
But folk likit him weel.

Soutar B: July, Friday 16th:

Soutar A: With death in the breast, the body has to conserve its strength. (I've stopped even thinking about women.) The body maun come hame to itsel. Yet still the spirit goes out, forgetting the doom upon its flesh. I must finish sorting out my poems ...

Soutar **B:** Jim Finlayson stepped in after so many years, and his welcome took place quite naturally, as if he'd been here last week.

Soutar **A:** The other day, I realised that I no longer whistle or sing, not out of depression, but poor respiration.

Soutar **B:** August, Friday 13th, 1943:

Soutar **A:** Why do we wish to be remembered when none remain who looked upon our face?

Soutar **B:** It is a last acknowledgement that we need to be loved, to keep our unseen presence within the borders of day.

Soutar **A:** But to be remembered we must have given our fellows a gift of service, however small.

Soutar **A:** D. B. Low my medico
Pronounced with bedside gravity:

Soutar **B:** "I fear, I fear, that I can hear
The echo of a cavity."

Soutar **B:** Ten days or so, and D. B. Low
With specialist suavity
Soon searches out, beyond a doubt,
The echo of a cavity.

Soutar **A:** Ten days or so, and so, and so,
I find my thoughts' depravity
Begin to hint there is small stint
Of treasure in this cavity ...

Soutar **B:** September, Sunday 12th:

Soutar **A:** I can no longer pull myself up or push myself from side to side – I've weakened a lot lately. And my breathlessness makes me irritable – a man of my age on the verge o tears – actin like a bairn. I must try to control this – a lot of pride to be knocked out of me yet.

Soutar **B:** If we can appreciate the world with a little gladness, the wish to live remains.

Soutar **A:** But when the pain is so strong that we withdraw and merely endure, we must ask: If the world is now a nothingness let us pass away from it?

Soutar **B:** *(moving closer)* No indication yet of the stoic calm I imagined I'd achieve as the end approaches.

Soutar **A:** I hope I shall be remembered as a poet, so that at least my folks aren't forgotten – they've done so much for me and received so little in return.

Soutar B: October, Friday 8th:

Soutar A: My body and soul cry out for change and refreshment – to feel the earth washed clean again, a sense of freedom and the return of joy.

Soutar B: And if I, in this privileged position, can have so intense longings – what agonies of desire for the millions of destitute folk on the continent.

Soutar B: *(moving to behind the bed)* October, Thursday 14th 1943 – the last entry:

Soutar A: During spells of drowsiness I find I'm getting satisfaction from speaking out a sentence in a deep voice. Something happens – I imagine someone is in the room – I ask a question as if people kent ma thoughts. Last night I must have been talking quite a lot – the folks said they heard me making noises about 1.30 ...

Another voice, female, reads or sings:

> Whaur yon broken brig hings owre;
> Whaur yon water makes nae soun';
> Babylon blaws by in stour;
> Gang doun wi' a sang, gang doun.

> Deep, owre deep, for onie drouth:
> Wan eneuch an ye wud droun:
> Saut or seelfu', for the mouth,
> Gang doun wi' a sang, gang doun.

> Babylon blaws by in stour
> Whaur yon water maks nae soun':
> Darkness is your only door;
> gang doun wi a sang, gang doun.

Soutar A: *(rises. Both stand together. Both speak.)* Free at last!

An intensity of yellow light on Soutar A and Soutar B. Exit both, leaving the stage in light

Curtain